THE
SECRET OF
SHAMBHALA

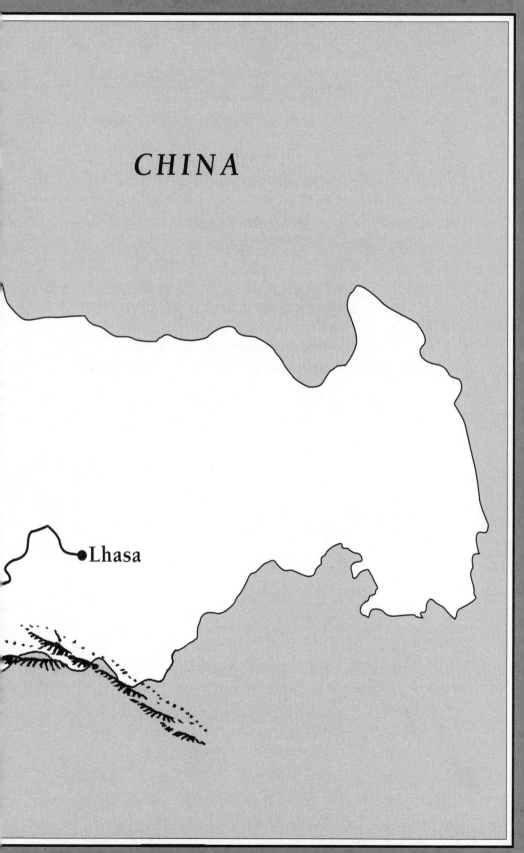

THE
SECRET OF
SHAMBHALA

*In Search of the
Eleventh Insight*

JAMES REDFIELD

WARNER BOOKS

A Time Warner Company

Warner Books, Inc., 1271 Avenue of the Americas,
New York, NY 10020

Visit our Web site at www.twbookmark.com

 A Time Warner Company

Printed in the United States of America
First Warner Books Printing: November 1999
10 9 8 7 6 5 4 3 2 1

ISBN: 0-446-52308-9
LCCN: 99-066555

For Megan and Kelly,
whose generation must evolve consciously.

ACKNOWLEDGMENTS

In the evolution of spiritual awareness, there are many heroes. A special thanks is in order to Larry Dossey, for his pioneering popularization of the scientific research on prayer and intention; also to Marilyn Schlitz, who continues to push the development of new studies on human intentionality for the Institute of Noetic Sciences. In nutrition, recognition must be given to the acid/ alkaline work of Theodore A. Baroody and Robert Young.

Personally, I must thank Albert Gaulden, John Winthrop Austin, John Diamond, and Claire Zion, who all continue to make special contributions to this work. And most of all, a special thanks to Salle Merrill Redfield, whose intuition and faith-power serve as a constant reminder of the mystery.

AUTHOR'S NOTE

When I wrote *The Celestine Prophecy* and *The Tenth Insight,* I was firmly convinced that human culture was evolving through a series of insights into life and spirituality, insights that could be described and documented. All that has occurred since has only deepened this belief.

We are becoming fully conscious of a higher spiritual process operating behind the scenes in life, and in doing so, we are leaving behind a materialistic worldview that reduces life to survival, gives a pittance to Sunday religion, and uses toys and distractions to push away the true awe of being alive.

What we want instead is a life filled with mysterious coincidences and sudden intuitions that allude to a special path for ourselves in this existence, to a particular pursuit of information and expertise—as though some intended destiny is pushing to emerge. This kind of life is like a detective story into ourselves, and the clues soon lead us forward through one insight after another.

We discover that a real experience of the divine within awaits us, and if we can find this connection, our lives are infused with even more clarity and intuition. We begin to catch visions of our destiny, of some mission that we can accomplish, provided we work through our distracting habits, treat others with a certain ethic, and stay true to our heart.

In fact, with the Tenth Insight, this perspective expands even more to include the full scope of history and culture. At some level, all of us know that we come from another heavenly place into this earthly dimension to participate in one overall goal: to slowly, generation by generation, create a completely spiritual culture on this planet.

Yet even as we grasp this invigorating insight, a new one, the Eleventh, is arriving. Our thoughts and attitudes count in making our dreams come true. In fact, I believe we are on the verge of understanding, finally, the way our mental intentions, our prayers, even our secret opinions and assumptions influence not only our own success in life but the success of others as well.

Based on my own experience, and on what is happening around us, this book is offered as an illustration of this next step in awareness. It is my belief that this insight is already emerging out there, swirling among thousands of late-night spiritual discussions, and hidden just below the hatred and fear that still mark our era. As before, our only responsibility is to live up to what we know, and then to reach out . . . and spread the word.

James Redfield
Summer 1999

CONTENTS

Then Nebuchadnezzar the king was astonished,
and rose up in haste and spake . . .
Did we not cast three men bound into the midst of the fire?
. . . Lo, I see four men loose, walking in the midst of the fire,
and they have no hurt, and the form
of the fourth is like the son of God . . .
Blessed be the God of Shadrach, Meshach, and Abednego
who hath sent his angel, and delivered his servants
that trusted in him.

—Book of Daniel

THE
SECRET OF
SHAMBHALA

1

FIELDS OF INTENTION

The phone rang and I just stared at it. The last thing I needed now was another distraction. I tried to push it from my mind, gazing out the window at the trees and wildflowers, hoping to lose myself in the array of fall colors in the woods around my house.

It rang again, and I got a vague but stirring image in my mind's eye of a person needing to talk with me. Quickly I reached over and answered it.

"Hello."

"It's Bill," a familiar voice said. Bill was an agronomy expert who had been helping me with my garden. He lived down the ridge only a few hundred yards.

"Listen, Bill, can I call you back later?" I said. "I've got this deadline."

"You haven't met my daughter, Natalie, yet, have you?"

"Excuse me?"

No reply.

"Bill?"

"Listen," he finally answered, "my daughter wants to talk with you. I think it might be important. I'm not quite sure how she knows, but she seems to be familiar with your work. She says she has some information about a place you'd be interested in. Some location in the north of Tibet? She says the people there have some important information."

"How old is she?" I asked.

Bill chuckled on the other end of the line. "She's only four-teen, but she's been saying some really interesting things lately. She was hoping she could talk with you this afternoon, before her soccer game. Any chance?"

I started to put him off, but the earlier image expanded and started to become clear in my mind. It seemed to be of the young girl and me talking somewhere near the big spring just up from her house.

"Yeah, okay," I said. "How about two p.m.?"

"That's perfect," Bill said.

On the walk over I caught sight of a new house across the valley on the north ridge. That makes almost forty, I thought. All in the last two years. I knew the word was out about the beauty of this bowl-shaped valley, but I really wasn't worried that the place would become overcrowded or that the amazing natural vistas would be destroyed. Nestled right up next to a national forest, we were ten miles from the closest town—too far away for most people. And the family who owned this land and was now selling selected house sites on the outer ridges seemed deter-mined to keep the serenity of the place unspoiled. Each house had to be low-slung and hidden amid the pines and sweet gums that defined the skyline.

What bothered me more was the preference for isolation ex-hibited by my neighbors. From what I could tell, most were char-acters of a sort, refugees from careers in various professions, who had carved out unique vocational niches that allowed them to now operate on flextime or travel on their own schedules as consultants—a freedom that was necessary if one was to live this far out in the wilderness.

The common bonds among all of us seemed to be a persistent idealism and the need to stretch our particular professions by an infusion of spiritual vision, all in the best Tenth Insight tradition. Yet almost everyone in this valley stayed to themselves, content to focus on their diverse fields without much attention to community or the need to build on our common vision. This was especially true among those of different religious persuasions. For some reason, the valley had attracted people holding a wide range of beliefs, including Buddhism, Judaism, both Catholic and Protestant Christianity, and Islam. And while there was no hostility of any kind by one religious group toward another, there wasn't a feeling of affinity either.

The lack of community concerned me because there were signs that a few of our kids were displaying some of the same problems seen in suburbia: too much time alone, too much video, and too much regard for the slights and put-downs at school. I was beginning to be concerned that there wasn't enough family and community in their lives to push these peer problems into the background and keep them in proper perspective.

Up ahead the path narrowed, and I had to make my way between two large boulders that edged right up to a sheer drop-off of about two hundred feet. Once past, I could hear the first gurgles of Phillips' Spring, named by the fur trappers that first set up a camp here in the late seventeenth century. The water trickled down several tiers of rocks into a lazy pool ten feet across that had originally been dug out by hand. Successive generations had added features, such as apple trees up near the mouth and mortared stone to reinforce and deepen the pool. I walked up to the water and reached down to cup some in my hand, brushing a stick out of the way as I leaned forward. The stick kept moving, slithering up the rock face and into a hole.

"Cottonmouth!" I said aloud, stepping back and feeling the sweat pop out on my brow. There are still perils involved in living here in the wild, although not perhaps the ones that old man Phillips faced centuries ago, when you could turn a corner on the path one day and come face-to-face with a big cougar guarding her young, or worse, a pack of wild boars with three-inch tusks that would slit your leg wide open if you didn't get up a tree fast enough. If the day was going especially bad, you might even come upon an angry Cherokee or a displaced Seminole who was tired of finding some new settler on his favorite hunting grounds . . . and was harboring the conviction that a large bite of your heart would stem the European tide forever. No, everyone alive in that generation—Native Americans and Europeans alike—faced direct perils that tested one's mettle and courage in the moment.

Our generation seemed to be dealing with other problems, problems that are more related to our attitude toward life, and the constant battle between optimism and despair. Everywhere are the voices of doom these days, showing us factual evidence that the modern Western lifestyle can't be sustained, that the air is warming, the terrorists' arsenals growing, the forests dying, and the technology running wild into a kind of virtual world that makes our kids crazy—and threatens to take us further and further into distraction and aimless surrealism.

Countering this viewpoint, of course, are the optimists, who claim that history has been filled with doomsayers, that all our problems can be handled by the same technology that produced these perils, and that the human world has only begun to reach its potential.

I stopped and looked out at the valley again. I knew that the

Celestine Vision lay somewhere in between these poles. It encompassed a belief in sustainable growth and humane technology, but only if pursued by an intuitive move toward the sacred, and an optimism based on a spiritual vision of where the world can go.

One thing was certain. If those who believe in the power of vision were to make a difference, it had to begin right now, when we're poised in the mystery of the new millennium. The fact of it still awed me. How did we get lucky enough to be the ones alive when not only a century changed but a thousand-year period as well. Why us? Why this generation? I got the feeling that larger answers were still ahead.

I looked around the spring for a moment, half expecting Natalie to be up here somewhere. I was sure this was the intuition I'd had. She'd been here at the spring, only I seemed to be looking at her through a window of some kind. It was all very confusing.

When I arrived at her house, there seemed to be no one home. I walked onto the deck of the dark brown A-frame and knocked on the door loudly. No answer. Then, as I glanced around the left side of the house, something grabbed my attention. I was looking down a rock pathway that led past Bill's huge vegetable garden and up to a small grassy meadow on the very top of the ridge. Had the light changed?

I looked up at the sky, trying to figure out what had occurred. I had seen a shift in the light in the meadow as though the sun had been behind a cloud and then had suddenly peaked out, illuminating that specific area. But there were no clouds. I strolled up to the meadow and found the young girl sitting at the edge of the grass. She was tall and dark-haired, wearing a blue soccer uniform, and as I approached, she jerked around, startled.

"Didn't mean to scare you," I said.

She looked away for a moment in the shy way a teenager

might, so I squatted down to be at her eye level and introduced myself.

She looked back at me with eyes much older than I expected.

"We aren't living the Insights here," she said.

I was taken aback. "What?"

"The Insights. We aren't living them."

"What do you mean?"

She looked at me sternly. "I mean, we haven't figured it out completely. There's more that we have to know."

"Well, it's not that easy . . ."

I stopped. I couldn't believe I was being confronted by a four-teen-year-old like this. For an instant a flash of anger swept across me. But then Natalie smiled—not a large smile, just an expression at the edges of her mouth that made her endearing. I relaxed and sat down on the ground.

"I believe the Insights are real," I said. "But they aren't easy. It takes time."

She wasn't letting up. "But there are people who are living them now."

I looked at her for a moment. "Where?"

"In central Asia. The Kunlun Mountains. I've seen it on the map." She sounded excited. "You have to go there. It's important. There's something changing. You have to go there now. You have to see it."

As she said this, the expression on her face looked mature, authoritative, like that of a forty-year-old. I blinked hard, not believing what I was seeing.

"You have to go there," she repeated.

"Natalie," I said, "I'm not sure where you mean. What kind of place is it?"

She looked away.

"You said you saw it on the map. Can you show it to me?"

She ignored my question, looking distracted. "What . . . what time is it?" she asked slowly, stuttering.

"Two-fifteen."

"I gotta go."

"Wait, Natalie, this place you were talking about. I—"

"I gotta meet the team," she said. "I'm going to be late."

She was walking fast now, and I struggled to reach her. "What about this place in Asia, can you remember exactly where it is?"

As she glanced back at me over her shoulder, I saw only the expression of a fourteen-year-old girl with her mind on soccer.

Back at home I found myself totally distracted. What was that all about? I stared at my desk, unable to concentrate. Later I took a long walk and a swim in the creek, finally deciding to call Bill in the morning and get to the bottom of the mystery. I retired early.

At about 3:00 A.M. something woke me. The room was dark. The only light was seeping in around the base of the window blinds. I listened intently, hearing nothing but the usual sounds of the night: an intermittent chorus of crickets, the occasional drone of bullfrogs down by the creek, and far away, the low bark of a dog.

I thought about getting up and locking the doors of the house, something I seldom ever did. But I shrugged off the idea, content to let myself ease back into sleep. I would have faded away altogether, except that in my last sleepy glance about the room, I noticed something different at the window. There was more light outside than before.

I sat up and looked again. There was definitely more light coming in around the blinds. I pulled on some pants and walked over to the window and parted the wooden slats. Everything appeared normal. Where had that light come from?

Suddenly I heard a light knocking behind me. Someone was in the house.

"Who's there?" I asked without thinking.

No answer.

I walked out of the bedroom and into the hall that led to the living room, thinking about going to the closet and getting out my snake rifle. But I realized the key to the closet was back in the dresser drawer by the bed. Instead I carefully walked on.

Without warning, a hand touched my shoulder.

"Shhhhh, it's Wil."

I recognized the voice and nodded. When I reached for the light on the wall, he stopped me, then walked across the room and looked out through the window. As he moved, I realized that something about him was different from the last time I had seen him. He was somehow less graceful, and his features seemed completely ordinary, not slightly luminous as before.

"What are you looking for?" I asked. "What's going on? You scared me half to death."

He walked back toward me. "I had to see you. Everything has changed. I'm back where I was."

"What do you mean?"

He smiled at me. "I think all this is supposed to be happening, but I can no longer enter the other dimensions mentally, the way I could. I can still raise my energy to some degree, but I'm now firmly here in this world." He looked away for an instant. "It's almost as though what we did in understanding the Tenth Insight was just a taste, a preview, a glimpse of the future like in a near-death experience, and now it's over. Whatever we're to do now, we have to do right here on this Earth."

"I never could do it again anyway," I said.

Wil looked me in the eye. "You know, we've received a lot of information about human evolution, about paying attention, about being guided forward by intuition and the coincidences. We've been given a mandate to hold a new vision, all of us. Only we aren't making it happen at the level we can. Something in our knowledge is still missing."

He paused for a minute and then said, "I'm not sure why yet, but we have to go to Asia . . . somewhere near Tibet. Something is happening there. Something we have to know."

I was startled. Young Natalie had said the same thing.

Wil walked back to the window again, peering out.

"Why do you keep looking out the window?" I asked. "And why did you slip into the house? Why didn't you just knock? What's going on?"

"Probably nothing," he replied. "I just thought I was being followed earlier today. I couldn't be sure."

He walked back toward me. "I can't explain everything now. I'm not even sure myself of what is happening. But there is a place in Asia we must find. Can you meet me at the Hotel Himalaya in Kathmandu on the sixteenth?"

"Wait a minute! Wil, I have things to do here. I'm committed to . . ."

Wil looked at me with an expression I've never seen on anyone's face but his, a pure mixture of adventure and total intent. "It's okay," he said. "If you're not there on the sixteenth, you're not there. Just be sure if you come that you stay perfectly alert. Something will occur."

He was serious about giving me the choice, but he was smiling broadly.

I looked away, unamused. I didn't want to do this.

* * *

The next morning I decided I would tell no one where I was going except Charlene. The only problem was that she was on an assignment out of the country and it was impossible to reach her directly. All I could do was leave her an E-mail.

I walked over to my computer and sent it, wondering, as I always did, about the security of the Internet. Hackers can get into the most secure corporate and government computers. How hard would it be to intercept E-mail messages . . . especially when one remembers that the Internet was originally set up by the Defense Department as a link to their research confidants at major universities? Is the whole Internet monitored? I shook off the concern, concluding that I was being silly. Mine was one message among tens of millions. Who would care?

While I was on the computer, I made travel arrangements to arrive in Kathmandu, Nepal, on the sixteenth and stay at the Himalaya. I would have to leave in two days, I thought, barely enough time to make preparations.

I shook my head. Part of me was fascinated with the idea of going to Tibet. I knew that its geography was one of the most beautiful and mysterious in the world. But it was also a country under the repressive control of the Chinese government, and I knew it could be a dangerous place. My plan was to go only as far with this adventure as felt safe. No more getting in over my head and letting myself be pulled into something I couldn't control.

Wil had left my home as quickly as he had arrived, without telling me anything more, and my mind was full of questions. What did he know of this place near Tibet? And why was an adolescent girl telling me to go there? Wil was being very cautious. Why? I wasn't going a step beyond Kathmandu until I found out.

When the day came, I tried to stay very alert through the long flights to Frankfurt, New Delhi, and then Kathmandu, but nothing of note occurred. At the Himalaya, I checked in under my own name and put my things in the room, then began to look around, ending up at the lobby restaurant. Sitting there, I expected Wil to walk in any moment, but nothing happened. After an hour the idea of going to the pool came to mind, so I hailed a bellman and found out it was outside. It would be slightly chilly, but the sun was bright, and I knew the fresh air would help me adjust to the altitude.

I walked out the exit and found the pool in between the L-shaped wings of the building. There were more people there than I would have imagined, although few were talking. As I took a chair at one of the tables, I noticed that the people sitting around me—Asians mostly, with a few Europeans scattered about—seemed to be either stressed-out or very homesick. They frowned at each other and snapped at the hotel attendants for drinks and papers, avoiding eye contact at all cost.

Gradually my mood began to decline as well. Here I was, I thought, cooped up in one more hotel halfway around the world, without a friendly face anywhere. I took a breath and again remembered Wil's admonition to stay alert, reminding myself that he was talking about watching for the subtle twists and turns of synchronicity, those mysterious coincidences that could pop up in a second to push one's life in a new direction.

Perceiving this mysterious flow, I knew, remained the central experience of real spirituality, direct evidence that something deeper was operating behind the scenes of the human drama. The problem has always been the sporadic nature of this perception; it comes along for a while to entice us and then, just as quickly, disappears.

As I looked around the area, my eyes fell on a tall man with black hair who was walking out of the hotel door heading straight for me. He was dressed in tan slacks and a stylish white sweater and carried a folded newspaper under his arm. He walked along the path through the loungers and sat at a table directly to my right. As he took out his newspaper, he looked around and nodded to me, smiling radiantly. Then he called an attendant over and ordered some water. He was Asian in appearance, but he spoke in fluent English with no detectable accent.

When his water arrived, he signed the ticket and began to read. There was something immediately attractive about this man, but I couldn't put my finger on what it was. He just radiated a pleasant demeanor and energy, and periodically he would stop reading and look around with a wide smile. At one point he made eye contact with one of the crabby gentlemen directly in front of me.

I was half expecting the sullen man to look away quickly, but instead he smiled back at the dark-haired man and they began to engage in light conversation in what sounded like Nepalese. At one point they even burst out laughing. Attracted by the conversation, several other people at nearby tables became amused, and one said something that created another round of laughter.

I looked out on the scene with interest. Something was happening here, I thought. The mood around me was changing.

"My God," the dark-haired man stammered, looking in my direction. "Have you seen this?"

I looked around. Everybody else seemed to have returned to their reading, and he was pointing to something in the paper and moving his chair around to get closer to me.

"They've released another prayer study," he added. "It's fascinating."

"What did they find?" I asked.

"They were studying the effect of praying for people who have medical problems, and found that patients who received regular prayers from others had fewer complications and got well faster, even when they weren't aware that prayers were being said. It's undeniable proof that the force of prayer is real. But they also found something else. They found that the most effective prayer of all was structured not as a request, but as an affirmation."

"I'm not sure what you mean," I said.

He was staring at me with crystal-blue eyes. "They set up the study to test two types of prayer. The first was just asking God, or the divine, to intervene, to help a sick person. The other was to simply affirm, with faith, that God will help the person. Do you see the difference?"

"I'm still not sure."

"A prayer that asks God to intervene assumes that God *can* intervene but only if he decides to honor our request. It assumes that we have no role except to ask. The other form of prayer assumes that God is ready and willing but has set up the laws of human existence so that whether the request is fulfilled depends in some part on the certainty of our belief that it will be done. So our prayer must be an affirmation that voices this faith. In the study, this kind of prayer proved to be most effective."

I nodded. I was beginning to get it.

The man looked away as though thinking to himself and then continued. "All the great prayers in the Bible are not requests, they are affirmations. Think of the Lord's Prayer. It goes, 'Thy will be done on Earth as it is in Heaven. Give us this day our daily bread, and forgive us our trespasses.' It doesn't say please can we have some food, and it doesn't say please can we be forgiven. It merely affirms that these things are ready to happen already, and by faithfully assuming that they will, we make it so."

He paused again, as though expecting a question, still smiling.

I had to chuckle. His good mood was so contagious.

"Some scientists are theorizing," he went on, "that these findings also imply something else, something that has a profound significance for every person alive. They maintain that if our expectations, our faithful assumptions, are what makes prayer work, then each of us is beaming a force of prayer-energy out into the world all the time, whether we realize it or not. Do you see how this is true?"

He continued without waiting for me to answer. "If prayer is an affirmation based on our expectations, our faith, then all our expectations have a prayer effect. We are, in fact, praying all the time for some kind of future for ourselves and others, we just aren't fully aware of it."

He looked at me as though he had just dropped a bombshell.

"Can you imagine?" he continued. "Science is now confirming the assertions of the most esoteric mystics of every religion. They all say we have a mental and spiritual influence on what happens to us in life. Remember the scriptures about how faith the size of a mustard seed can move mountains. What if this ability is the secret of true success in life, of creating true community." His eyes twinkled as though he knew more than he was saying. "We all have to figure out how this works. It's time."

I was smiling back at this man, intrigued by what he was saying, still amazed at the transformation in the mood around the pool, when I instinctively glanced around to the left in the way we do when we feel someone looking at us. I caught one of the pool attendants staring at me from the entrance door. When our eyes met, he quickly looked away and began to walk back along the sidewalk that led to an elevator.

"Excuse me, sir," came a voice from behind me.

When I looked around, I realized it was another attendant.

"May I serve you a drink?" he asked.

"No . . . thank you," I replied. "I'll wait awhile.

When I looked back toward the man on the sidewalk, he was gone. For a moment I surveyed the area, looking for him. When I finally looked over to my right where the dark-haired man had been sitting, he was gone too.

I got up and asked the man at the table in front of me if he had seen which way the man with the paper had walked. He shook his head and looked away curtly.

For the rest of the afternoon I stayed in my room. The events at the pool were disconcerting. Who was the man telling me about prayer? Was there a synchronicity involved with this information? And why was the attendant staring at me? And where was Wil?

Around dusk, after a long nap, I ventured out again, deciding to walk down the street a few blocks to an outdoor restaurant I heard one of the guests mention.

"Very close. Perfectly safe," the bespectacled concierge told me when I asked him how to get there. "No problem."

I walked out of the lobby into the fading light, keeping an eye out for Wil. The street was crowded with people and I pushed my way through. When I arrived at the restaurant, I was given a small corner table next to a four-foot-high wrought-iron fence that separated the dining area from the street. I ate a leisurely dinner and read an English newspaper, keeping the table for more than an hour.

At one point I grew uncomfortable. I felt as though I was being watched again, only I couldn't see anyone looking. I gazed around at the other tables, but no one seemed to be paying me the slightest attention. Standing up, I peered over the fence at the people on the street. Nothing. Struggling to shake the feeling, I paid the check and walked back toward the hotel.

As I neared the entrance, I caught sight of a man at the edge of a row of bushes about twenty feet away to my left. Our eyes met and he took a step toward me. I looked away and was walking past when I realized it was the attendant I had caught looking at me at the pool, only he was now dressed in sneakers and jeans with a plain blue shirt. He appeared to be about thirty, with very serious eyes. I hurried on by.

"Excuse me, sir," he called out.

I continued to walk.

"Please," he said. "I must speak with you."

I moved a few yards farther so that I would be in sight of the doorman and bell staff, then asked, "What is it?"

He moved closer, half bowing. "You are someone I believe I am here to meet. You know Mr. Wilson James?"

"Wil? Yes. Where is he?"

"He is unable to come. He asked me to meet you instead." He offered his hand and I took it reluctantly, telling him my name.

"I am Yin Doloe," he replied.

"Are you an employee here at the hotel?" I asked.

"No, I'm sorry. A friend works here. I borrowed a jacket from him so I could look around. I wanted to see if you were here."

I looked at him closely. My instincts told me he was telling the truth. But why the secrecy? Why didn't he just walk up to me at the pool and ask who I was?

"Why has Wil been delayed?" I asked.

"I am not sure. He asked me to meet you and take you on to Lhasa. His plan, I believe, is to meet us there."

I looked away. Things were beginning to feel ominous. I looked him over again, then said, "I'm not sure I want to do that. Why hasn't Wil called me himself?"

"I'm sure there is an important reason," Yin replied, taking a step toward me. "Wil was very insistent that I bring you to him. He needs you."

Yin's eyes were pleading. "Could we leave tomorrow?"

"Let's do this," I said. "Why don't you come inside and we'll have a cup of coffee and talk about the situation?"

He was looking around as though afraid of something. "Please, I'll come back at eight tomorrow morning. Wil has already arranged a flight and visa for you." He smiled, then scurried away before I could protest.

At 7:55 I walked out the door of the main lobby with only one satchel. The hotel had agreed to store everything else. My plan was to be back within the week—unless, of course, something strange happened once I left with Yin. In that case, I would be back immediately.

Exactly on time, Yin drove up in an old Toyota and we headed toward the airport. On the way over, he was cordial, but he continued to plead ignorance as to what was going on with Wil. I considered telling him what Natalie had said about the mysterious place in central Asia and what Wil had told me that night in my bedroom, just to see Yin's reaction. But I decided against it. Better to just watch Yin closely, I thought, and see how things felt at the airport.

At the ticket desk, I found that a seat had indeed been purchased in my name for a flight to Lhasa. I looked around and tried to feel out the situation. Everything seemed normal. Yin was smiling, obviously in a good mood. Unfortunately the ticket clerk was not. She could speak only a little English and was very demanding. When she asked for my passport, I became ever more irritated and snapped back at her. At one point she stopped and glared at me, as though she was going to refuse to issue the tickets altogether.

Yin quickly stepped in and talked to her in a calm voice in her native Nepalese. After a few minutes her demeanor began to change. She never looked at me again, but she spoke pleasantly to Yin, actually laughing at something he said. A few minutes later we had our tickets and boarding passes and were sitting at a small table in a coffee shop near our gate. There was the strong smell of cigarettes everywhere.

"You have much anger," Yin said. "And you don't use your energy very well."

I was taken aback. "What are you talking about?"

He looked at me with kindness. "I mean, you did nothing to help the woman at the counter with her mood."

I immediately knew what he was getting at. In Peru the Eighth Insight had described a method of uplifting others by focusing on their faces in a particular way.

"You know the Insights?" I asked.

Yin nodded, still looking at me. "Yes," he said. "But there is more."

"Remembering to send energy is not that easy," I added defensively.

In a very deliberate tone, Yin said, "But you must realize that you were already influencing her with your energy anyway, whether you know it or not. The important thing is how you set your . . . field of . . . of . . ." Yin was struggling to find the English word. "Field of *intention*," he said finally. "Your prayer-field."

I looked at him hard. Yin seemed to be describing prayer in the same way the dark-haired man had earlier.

"What are you talking about exactly?" I asked.

"Have you ever been in a room of people where the energy and mood were low, and then someone comes in who lifts everyone's energy immediately, just by entering the room? This person's energy field goes out ahead of him or her and touches everyone else."

"Yeah," I said. "I know what you mean."

His look penetrated me. "If you are going to find Shambhala, you must learn how to do this consciously."

"Shambhala? What are you talking about?"

Yin's face grew pale, exuding an expression of embarrassment. He shook his head, apparently feeling as though he had overstepped himself and let something out of the bag.

"Never mind," he said lowly. "It is not my place. Wil must explain this." The line was forming to enter the plane, and Yin turned away and moved toward the ticket steward.

I was wracking my brain, trying to place the word "Shambhala." Finally it came to me. Shambhala was the mythical community of Tibetan Buddhist lore, the one that the stories about Shangri-La had been based on.

I caught Yin's eye. "That place is a myth . . . right?"

Yin just handed the steward his ticket and walked down the aisle.

On the flight to Lhasa, Yin and I sat in different sections of the plane, giving me time to think. All I knew was that Shambhala was of great significance to Tibetan Buddhists, whose ancient writings described it as a holy city of diamonds and gold, filled with adepts and lamas—and hidden somewhere in the vast uninhabitable regions of northern Tibet or China. More recently, though, most Buddhists seemed to speak of Shambhala merely in symbolic terms, as representing a spiritual state of mind, not a real location.

I reached over and pulled a travel brochure of Tibet from the pouch on the seat back, hoping to get a renewed sense of its geography. Lying between China to the north and India and Nepal to the south, Tibet is basically a large plateau with few areas lower than six thousand feet. At its southern border are the towering Himalayas, including Mount Everest, and on the northern border just inside China are the vast Kunlun Mountains. In between are deep gorges, wild rivers, and hundreds of square miles of rocky tundra. From the map, eastern Tibet seemed to be the most fertile and populated, while the north and west looked sparse and mountainous, with few roads, all of them gravel.

Apparently there are only two major routes into western Tibet—the northern road, used mostly by truckers, and the southern road, which skirts the Himalayas and is used by pilgrims from all over the region to reach the sacred sites of Everest, Lake Manasarovar, and Mount Kailash, and farther on to the mysterious Kunluns.

I looked up from my reading. As we flew along at thirty-five thousand feet, I began to sense a distinct shift in temperature and energy outside. Below me, the Himalayas rose in frozen, rocky spires, framed by a clear blue sky. We practically flew right over the top of Mount Everest as we passed into the airspace of Tibet—the land of snows, the rooftop of the world. It was a nation of seekers, inward travelers, and as I looked down at the green valleys and rocky plains surrounded by mountains, I couldn't help being awed by its mystery. Too bad it was now being brutally administered by a totalitarian government. What, I wondered, was I doing here?

I looked back at Yin seated four rows behind me. It bothered me that he was being so secretive. I made up my mind, again, to be very cautious. I would not go any farther than Lhasa without a full explanation.

When we arrived at the airport, Yin resisted all my inquiries about Shambhala, repeating his assertion that soon we would be met by Wil, at which point I would learn everything. We caught a taxi and headed toward a small hotel near the center of town, where Wil would be waiting.

I caught Yin staring at me.

"What?" I asked.

"I was just checking to see how you are adjusting to the altitude," Yin said. "Lhasa is twelve thousand feet above sea level. You must take it easy for a while."

I nodded, appreciating his concern, but in the past I had always adapted easily to high altitudes. I was about to mention this to Yin when I caught sight of a huge, fortress-like structure in the distance.

"This is the Potala Palace," Yin said. "I wanted you to see it. It was the Dalai Lama's winter home before he was exiled. It now symbolizes the struggle of the Tibetan people against the Chinese occupation."

He looked away and remained silent until the car stopped not in front of the hotel, but down the street a hundred feet.

"Wil should be here already," Yin said as he opened the door. "Wait in the taxi. I'll go in and check."

But instead of getting out, he stopped and stared at the entrance. I saw his look and gazed in that direction myself. The street was busy with Tibetan pedestrians and a few tourists, but all seemed normal. Then my eyes fell on a short, Chinese man near the corner of the building. He held a paper of some kind, but his eyes were carefully surveying the area.

Yin looked toward the cars parked on the curb across the street from the man. His eyes stopped on an old brown sedan containing several men in suits.

Yin said something to the taxi driver, who looked nervously at us in the rearview mirror and drove toward the next intersection. As we drove on, Yin bent over so as not to be seen by the men in the car.

"What's going on?" I asked.

Yin ignored me, telling the driver to turn left and head farther into the center of the city.

I grabbed his arm. "Yin, tell me what's going on. Who were those men?"

"I don't know," he said. "But Wil would not be there. There is one other place I think he would go. Watch and see if we are being followed."

I looked behind us as Yin gave the taxi driver more instructions. Several cars came up behind us but then turned off. There was no sign of the brown sedan.

"Do you see anyone back there?" Yin asked, turning to look for himself.

"I don't think so," I replied.

I was about to question Yin again about what was happening when I noticed that his hands were shaking. I took a good look at his face. It was pale and covered with sweat. I realized that he was terrified. The sight sent a chill of fear through my own body.

Before I could speak, Yin pointed out a parking place for the taxi driver and pushed me out of the car with my satchel, leading me down a side street and then into a narrow alley. After walking a hundred feet or so, we leaned against the wall of a building and waited for several minutes, our eyes glued to the entrance of the street we had just left. Neither of us spoke a word.

When it appeared as though we were not being followed, Yin

proceeded down the alley to the next building and knocked several times. There was no answer, but the lock on the door mysteriously opened from the inside.

"Wait here," Yin said, opening the door. "I'll be back."

He moved silently into the building and shut the door. When I heard it lock, a wave of panic filled me. Now what? I thought. Yin was scared. Was he abandoning me out here? I looked back down the alley toward the crowded street. This was exactly what I had feared most. Someone seemed to be looking for Yin, and maybe Wil too. I had no idea what I might be getting involved in.

Perhaps it would be best if Yin did vanish, I thought. That way I could run back to the street and hide among the crowds until I found my way back to the airport. What else could I do then but go back home? I would be absolved of all responsibility to look for Wil or do anything else on this misadventure.

The door suddenly opened, Yin slid out, and the door was quickly locked.

"Wil left a message," Yin said. "Come on."

We walked a bit farther down the alley and hid between two large trash bins as Yin opened an envelope and pulled out a note. I watched him as he read. His face seemed to grow even whiter. When he finished, he held the note out toward me.

"What does it say?" I demanded, grabbing the paper. I recognized Wil's handwriting as I read:

Yin, I'm convinced we are being allowed into Shambhala. But I must go on ahead. It is of utmost importance that you bring our American friend as far as you can. You know the dakini will guide you.

Wil

I looked at Yin, who glanced at me for a moment and then looked away. "What does he mean, 'allowed into Shambhala'? He means that figuratively, right? He doesn't think it's a real place, does he?"

Yin was staring at the ground. "Of course Wil thinks it's a real place," he whispered.

"Do you?" I asked.

He looked away, appearing as though the weight of the world had been placed on his shoulders.

"Yes . . . Yes . . . ," he said, "only it has been impossible for most people to ever conceive of this place, much less get there. Certainly you and I cannot . . ." His voice trailed off into silence.

"Yin," I said, "you have to tell me what's going on. What is Wil doing? Who are these men we saw at the hotel?"

Yin stared at me for a moment and then said, "I think they are Chinese intelligence officers."

"What?"

"I don't know what they are doing here. Apparently they have been alerted by all the activity and talk about Shambhala. Many of the lamas here realize that something is changing with this holy place. There has been much discussion.

"Changing how? Tell me."

Yin took a deep breath. "I wanted to let Wil explain this . . . but I guess now I must try. You must understand what Shambhala is. The people there are live human beings, born into this holy place, but they are of a higher evolutionary state. They help hold energy and vision for the whole world."

I looked away, thinking about the Tenth Insight. "They're spiritual guides of some kind?"

"Not like you think," Yin replied. "They aren't like family members or other souls in the afterlife that might be helping us from that dimension. They are human beings who live right here on this Earth. Those in Shambhala have an extraordinary community and live at a higher level of development. They model what the rest of the world will ultimately achieve."

"Where is this place?"

"I don't know."

"Do you know anyone who has seen it?"

"No. As a boy, I studied with a great lama, who declared one day that he was going to Shambhala, and after days of celebration, he left."

"Did he get there?"

"No one knows. He disappeared and was never seen again anywhere in Tibet."

"Then no one really knows whether it exists or not."

Yin was silent for a moment, then said, "We have the legends . . ."

"Who's we?"

He stared at me. I could tell that he was restricted by some kind of code of silence. "I cannot tell you that. Only the head of our sect, Lama Rigden, could choose to talk with you."

"What are the legends?"

"I can only tell you this: The legends are the sayings left by those who have attempted to reach Shambhala in the past. They are centuries old."

Yin was about to say something else when a sound toward the street drew our attention. We watched closely but saw no one.

"Wait here," Yin said.

Again Yin knocked on the door and disappeared inside. Just as quickly he emerged and walked over to an old, rusty Jeep with a ragged canvas top. He opened the door and waved for me to get in.

"Come on," he said. "We must hurry."

2

THE CALL OF SHAMBHALA

As Yin began to drive out of Lhasa, I was silent, looking out at the mountains and wondering what Wil had meant by his note. Why had he decided to go on alone? And who were the dakini? I was about to ask Yin when a Chinese military truck crossed at the intersection in front of us.

The sight gave me a jolt, and I felt a wave of nervousness begin to fill my body. What was I doing? We had just seen intelligence officers staking out the hotel where we were supposed to meet Wil. They might be looking for us.

"Wait a minute, Yin," I said. "I want to go to an airport. All this seems too dangerous for me."

Yin looked at me with alarm. "What about Wil?" he said. "You read the note. He needs you."

"Yeah, well, he's used to this kind of stuff. I'm not sure he would expect me to put myself in danger like this."

"You are already in danger. We must get out of Lhasa."

"Where are you going?" I asked.

"To Lama Rigden's monastery near Shigatse. It will be late when we get there."

"Is there a phone there?" I asked.

"Yes," Yin replied. "I believe so, if it's working."

I nodded and Yin turned back to concentrate on the road.

That's fine, I thought. It wouldn't hurt to get far away from here before making arrangements to get home.

For hours we bounced along on the badly paved highway, passing trucks and old cars along the way. The scenery was a mix of ugly industrial developments and beautiful vistas. Well after dark, Yin pulled up into the yard of a small, concrete block house. A big, woolly dog was tied to the side of a mechanic's garage to the right, barking at us furiously.

"Is this Lama Rigden's house?" I asked.

"No, of course not," Yin said. "But I know the people here. We can pick up some food and gasoline that we might need later. I'll be right back."

I watched as Yin walked up the board steps and knocked on the door. An older Tibetan woman came out and immediately pulled Yin into a full embrace. Yin pointed at me, smiled, and said something I couldn't understand. He waved for me, and I got out and walked into the house.

A moment later we heard the faint squeaks of car brakes outside. Yin darted across the room and pulled back the curtains to look. I stood right behind him. In the darkness, I could see a black unmarked car sitting on the side of the road across from the rutted driveway, a hundred feet away.

"Who is that?" I asked.

"I don't know," Yin replied. "Go out and get our packs, quickly."

I looked at him questioningly.

"It's okay," he said. "Go get them, but hurry."

I walked out the door and over to the Jeep, trying not to look toward the car in the distance. I reached through the open window and grabbed my satchel and Yin's pack and then briskly walked back inside. Yin was still watching out the window.

"Oh my," he said suddenly, "they're coming."

A blast of car lights lit the window as the car raced toward the house. Grabbing his pack from me with one hand, Yin led the way out the back door and into the darkness.

"We must go this way," Yin yelled back at me as he led me up a path into a group of rocky foothills. I glanced back down at the house and, to my horror, saw plainclothes agents piling out of the car and encircling the residence. Another car we hadn't even seen sped around the side of the house, and several more men jumped out and began to run up the slope to our right. I knew if we kept going in the direction we were going, they would cut us off in minutes.

"Yin, wait a minute," I said in a loud whisper. "They're heading us off."

He stopped and put his face very close to mine in the darkness.

"To the left," he said. "We'll go around them."

As he said that, I caught sight of the other agents running in that direction. If we followed Yin's route, they would see us for sure.

I looked straight up the most rugged part of the incline. Something caught my eye: A dim patch of the trail was perceptibly lighter.

"No, we have to go straight up," I said instinctively, and headed in that direction. Yin lagged behind me for an instant and then hurriedly followed. We made our way up the rocks, with the agents closing in from the right.

At the top of a rise, an agent seemed to be right on top of us and we ducked between two large boulders. The area around us was still perceptibly lighter. The man was no more than thirty feet away, moving around to where he would soon see us clearly. Then, as he approached the edges of the slight glow, seconds from seeing us, he abruptly stopped, started to walk forward again, then stopped again, as if suddenly having other ideas. Without taking another step, he turned and ran back down the hill.

After a few moments I asked Yin in a whisper if he thought the agent had seen us.

"No," Yin replied. "I do not think so. Come on."

We climbed the hill for another ten minutes before stopping on a stony precipice to look back down at the house. We could see more official-looking cars driving up. One was an older police car with a blinking red light. The scene filled me with terror. No doubt about it now, these people were after us.

Yin was also looking anxiously toward the house, his hands again shaking.

"What are they going to do to your friend?" I asked, horrified at what he might say.

Yin looked at me with tears and fury in his eyes, then led the way farther up the hill.

We walked for several more hours, making our way by the light of a quarter-moon that was periodically obscured by clouds. I wanted to ask about the legends Yin had mentioned, but he remained angry and sullen. At the top of the hill, Yin stopped and announced that we must rest. As I sat down on a nearby rock, he walked off into the darkness a dozen feet or so and stood with his back toward me.

"Why were you so sure," he asked without turning around, "that we should climb straight up the hill back there?"

I took a breath. "I saw something," I stammered. "The area was lighter somehow. It seemed the way to go."

He turned and walked over and sat down on the ground across from me. "Have you seen such a thing before?"

I tried to shake away my anxiety. My heart was pounding and I could barely talk.

"Yeah, I have," I said. "Several times recently."

He looked away and was silent.

"Yin, do you know what is happening?"

"The legends would say we are being helped."

"Helped by whom?"

Again he just looked away.

"Yin, tell me what you know about this."

He did not respond.

"Is it the dakini that Wil mentioned in his note?"

Still no response.

I felt a rush of anger. "Yin! Tell me what you know."

He stood up quickly and glared at me. "Some things we are forbidden to speak of. Don't you understand? Just mentioning the names of these beings frivolously can leave a man mute for years, or blind. They are the guardians of Shambhala."

He stormed over to a flat rock, spread his jacket, and lay down.

I felt exhausted too, unable to think.

"We must sleep," Yin said. "Please, you will know more to-morrow."

I looked at him for a moment longer, then lay down on the rock where I was sitting and fell into a deep sleep.

* * *

I was awakened by a shaft of light rising between two snowy peaks in the distance. Looking around, I realized that Yin was gone. I jumped up and searched the immediate area, my body aching all over. Yin was nowhere I could see.

Damn, I thought. I had no way of knowing where I was. A deep wave of anxiety rushed through me. I waited for thirty minutes, looking out at the brown, rocky hills with little valleys of green grass, and still he had not returned. Then I stood up again and noticed for the first time that down the slope about four hundred feet was a gravel road. I grabbed my satchel and walked down through the rocks until I reached the road and then headed north. As best I could remember, that was the direction back toward Lhasa.

I hadn't gone a half mile before I noticed that there were four or five people less than a hundred paces behind me heading in the same direction. I immediately left the road and moved well up into the rocks so that I would be hidden but could still watch them pass. When they reached me, I realized that it was a family, made up of an old man, a man and a woman of about thirty, and two teenage boys. They were carrying large sacks, and the younger man was pulling a cart filled with possessions. They looked like refugees.

I thought about approaching them and at least finding out which way to go, but I decided against it. I was afraid they might report me later, and so I let them go by. I waited another twenty minutes, then carefully walked in the same direction. For about two miles the road weaved its way through the small rocky hills and plateaus, until in the distance, at the top of one of the hills, I could see a monastery. I moved off the road and climbed through the rocks until I was about two hundred yards below it. It was made of sandy-colored brick, with the flat roof painted brown, and had two wings, one on each side of a main building.

I could see no movement, and at first I thought the place was empty. But then the door at the front opened, and I saw a monk, adorned in a bright red robe, come out and begin to work in a garden near a lone tree to the right of the building.

He looked harmless enough, but I decided to take no chances. I walked back to the gravel road, crossed it, and made a wide berth around the left side of the monastery until I was well past. Then I carefully proceeded up the road again, stopping only to take off my parka. The sun was beating down now and it was surprisingly warm.

After about a mile, as I was about to crest a small rise in the road, I heard something. I ran into the rocks and listened. At first I thought it was a bird, but slowly I realized it was someone talking, far in the distance. Who?

Taking great care, I moved up through the rocks until I had a higher position, then peeked over at the small valley below. My heart froze. Below me was a gravel crossroads at which were parked three military jeeps. Perhaps a dozen soldiers stood around smoking cigarettes and talking. I backed away, keeping low, and walked the way I had come until I found a place to hide between two rocky mounds.

From there I heard something else in the distance out beyond the roadblock. It was a low drone at first and then a whirling, clapping sound I recognized. It was a helicopter.

Panicked, I ran through the rocks as fast as I could, away from the road. I crossed a small stream and slipped, drenching my pants up to the knees. I jumped up and started to run again when my foot slipped on one of the rocks and I careened down a hill, ripping my pants and gouging my leg. Struggling to my feet, I kept running, looking for a better place to hide.

As the helicopter closed, I bounded over another small rise and was looking back when someone grabbed me and pulled me down into a small gorge. It was Yin. We lay perfectly still as the large helicopter flew directly over us.

"It's a Z-9," Yin said. His face looked panicked, but I could tell he was also furious.

"Why did you leave where we were camped?" he half shouted.

"You left me!" I responded.

"I was gone less than an hour. You should have waited."

The fear and anger exploded in me. "Waited? Why didn't you tell me you were going?"

I wasn't through, but I could hear the helicopter turning in the distance.

"What are we going to do?" I asked Yin. "We can't stay here."

"Back to the monastery," he said. "That's where I was before."

I nodded, then raised up and looked for the helicopter. Luckily it was veering off to the north. At the same time, something else caught my eye. It was the monk I had seen earlier, moving down the ditch toward us.

He walked up to us and said something to Yin in Tibetan, then looked at me.

"Come, please," he said in English, grabbing me, pulling me toward the monastery.

When we arrived, we first walked through a side courtyard gate and past many Tibetans standing with bags and various belongings. Some of them looked very poor. Then we reached the main building of the monastery, and the monk opened the large wooden doors and led us through an entry room, where more Tibetans were gathered. As we walked by, I recognized one group; it was the family I had let pass me on the road earlier. They looked at me with warm eyes.

Yin saw me looking at them and questioned me about it, and I explained that I had seen them back on the road.

"They were there to lead you here," Yin said. "But you were too afraid to follow the synchronicity."

He glanced at me sternly and then continued to follow the monk into a small study with bookcases and desks and several prayer wheels. We were then seated around an ornately carved wooden table, where the monk and Yin carried on an extensive conversation in Tibetan.

"Let me see your leg," another monk asked in English from behind us. He carried a small basket filled with white bandages and several dropper bottles. Yin's face lit up.

"You two know each other?" I asked.

"Please," the monk said, offering his hand while bowing slightly. "I am Jampa."

Yin leaned toward me. "Jampa has been with Lama Rigden for over ten years."

"Who is Lama Rigden?"

Both Jampa and Yin looked at each other as though not sure how much to tell me. Finally Yin said, "I mentioned the legends to you earlier. Lama Rigden understands the legends more than any other person. He is one of the foremost experts on Shambhala."

"Tell me exactly what has happened," Jampa said to me as he dabbed some kind of salve on my scraped leg.

I looked at Yin, who nodded for me to comply.

"I must present what has happened to you to the Lama," Jampa clarified.

I proceeded to tell him everything that had occurred since arriving at Lhasa. When I finished, Jampa looked at me.

"What about before you came to Tibet? What had happened?"

I told him about my neighbor's daughter and about Wil.

He and Yin looked at each other.

"And what have you been thinking?" Jampa asked.

"I've been thinking that I'm in over my head here," I said. "I'm planning to head to the airport."

"No, that's not what I mean," Jampa said quickly. "This morning, when you discovered that Yin had left, what was your attitude, your state of mind?"

"I was scared. I just knew the Chinese would be on me in minutes. I tried to figure out how to get back to Lhasa."

Jampa turned and looked at Yin, frowning. "He doesn't know about the prayer-fields."

Yin shook his head and looked away.

"We've discussed it," I said. "But I'm not sure how it matters. What do you know about these helicopters? Are they after us?"

Jampa only smiled and told me not to worry, that I would be safe here. We were interrupted by several other monks delivering soup, bread, and tea. As we ate, my mind seemed to clear and I began to assess the situation. I wanted to know everything about what was going on. Right now.

I looked at Jampa with determination, and he returned my gaze with a profound warmth.

"I know you have many questions," he said. "Let me tell you as much as I can. We are a special sect here in Tibet. Not typical. For many centuries we have held the belief that Shambhala is a real place. We also hold the knowledge of the legends, verbal wisdom as old as the Kalachakra, which is devoted to the integration of all religious truth.

"Many of our lamas are in touch with Shambhala through their dreams. A few months ago, your friend Wil began to show up in Lama Rigden's dreams of Shambhala. A short time after that, Wil was led to this very monastery. Lama Rigden agreed to see him and found out Wil was also having dreams of Shambhala."

"What did Wil tell him?" I asked. "Where did he go?"

He shook his head. "I'm afraid you must wait and see if Lama Rigden will give you that information himself."

I looked at Yin, and he attempted to smile.

"What about the Chinese?" I asked Jampa. "How are they involved?"

Jampa shrugged. "We don't know. Perhaps they know something about what is happening."

I nodded.

"There's one more thing," Jampa said. "Apparently in all the dreams there appears another person. An American."

Jampa paused and bowed slightly. "Your friend Wil wasn't sure but he thought it was you."

After bathing and changing clothes in the room Jampa had provided, I walked out into the back courtyard. Several monks were working in a vegetable garden, as though the Chinese were of no concern. I looked out at the mountains and surveyed the sky. No helicopters anywhere.

"Would you like to sit on the bench up there?" a voice spoke from behind me. I turned and saw Yin walking out the door.

I nodded and we walked up several terraces filled with ornamental plants and vegetables until we reached a sitting area facing an elaborate Buddhist shrine. A large mountain range framed the horizon behind us, but toward the south we had a panoramic view of the countryside for miles. Many people were walking on the roads or pulling carts.

"Where is the Lama?" I asked.

"I don't know," Yin replied. "He has not yet agreed to see you."

"Why not?"

Yin shook his head. "I don't know."

"Do you think he knows where Wil is?"

Again Yin shook his head.

"Do you think the Chinese are still looking for us?" I asked.

Yin only shrugged, looking out into the distance.

"I'm sorry my energy is so bad," he said. "Please don't let it influence you. It's just that my anger overwhelms me. Since 1954, the Chinese have systematically set out to destroy the Tibetan culture. Look at those people walking out there. Many of them are farmers who are displaced because of economic initiatives the Chinese have mandated. Others are nomads who are starving because these policies have interrupted their way of life." He clenched both fists.

"The Chinese are doing the same thing Stalin did in Manchuria, importing thousands of outsiders, in this case ethnic Chinese, into Tibet to change the cultural balance and institute Chinese ways. They demand that our schools teach only the Chinese language."

"The people outside the gates of the monastery," I asked, "why do they come here?"

"Lama Rigden and the monks are working to help the poor, who are having the worst time with the transition of their culture. That is why the Chinese have left him alone. He helps solve the problems without agitating the populace against them."

Yin said this in a way that reflected a mild resentment against the Lama, and immediately he apologized.

"No," he said. "I didn't mean to imply that the Lama is cooperating too much. It's just that what the Chinese are doing is despicable." He clenched his fists again and hit his knees. "Many thought at first that the Chinese government would be respectful of Tibetan ways, that we could exist within the Chinese nation without losing everything. But the government is bent on destroying us. This is clear now and we must begin to make it more difficult for them."

"You mean try to fight them?" I asked. "Yin, you know you can't win that."

"I know, I know," he said. "I just get so angry when I think of what they are doing. Someday the warriors of Shambhala will ride out and defeat these monsters of evil."

"What?"

"It is a prophecy among my people." He looked at me and shook his head. "I know I must work on my anger. It collapses my prayer-field."

Abruptly he stood up and added, "I'll go ask Jampa if he has talked with the Lama. Please excuse me." He bowed slightly and left.

For a while I looked out at the Tibetan landscape, trying to comprehend fully the damage the Chinese occupation had done. At one point I even thought I heard another helicopter, but it was too far away to be sure. I knew Yin's anger was justified, and I thought for several more minutes about the realities of the political situation in Tibet. The thought of asking for a phone came back to mind, and I wondered how hard it would be to place an international call.

I was about to get up and head inside when I realized I felt tired, so I took a couple of deep breaths and tried to focus on the beauty around me. The snowcapped mountains and the green and brown colors of the landscape were stark and beautiful, and the sky was a rich blue with only a few clouds along the western horizon.

As I gazed out, I noticed that the two monks who were several tiers down below me were staring intently up in my direction. I glanced behind me to see if there was something up there, but I could see nothing unusual. I smiled back in their direction.

After a few minutes one of them walked up the stone steps toward me, carrying a basket full of hand tools. When he reached me, he nodded politely and began to weed a bed of flowers twenty feet to my right. Several minutes later he was joined by another monk, who began digging as well. Occasionally they would look over at me with inquiring eyes and deferential nods.

I took more deep breaths and focused on the far distance again, thinking about what Yin had said concerning his prayer-field. He was worried that his anger against the Chinese collapsed his energy. What did he mean by that?

Suddenly I began to feel the warmth of the sun and to sense its radiance more consciously, feeling a certain peacefulness I hadn't felt since coming here. I took another breath with my eyes closed and perceived something else, an unusually sweet fragrance like a bouquet of flowers. My first thought was that the monks had clipped some of the blooms off the plants they were working on and had placed them near me.

I opened my eyes and looked, but there were no flowers close by. I felt for a breeze that might have blown the fragrance over toward me, but there was none stirring. I noticed the monks had dropped their tools and were staring intensely at me with wide eyes and their mouths half-open, as though they had seen something strange. Again I looked behind me, trying to figure out what was going on. Upon noticing that they had disturbed me, they quickly gathered up their tools and baskets and almost ran down the path toward the monastery. I followed them with my eyes for a moment, watching their red robes flip and sway as they glanced back at me to see if I was watching.

*   *   *

As soon as I walked down and entered the monastery, I knew something was abuzz. The monks were all scurrying about and whispering to one another.

I walked down a hallway and into my own room, planning on asking Jampa for the use of a phone. My mood was better, but I was again questioning my own sense of self-preservation. I was being drawn further into what was happening here, instead of trying to get out of this country. Who knew what the Chinese might do if I was caught? Did they know my name? It might even be too late to leave by air.

I was about to get up and look for Jampa when he burst into the room.

"The Lama has agreed to see you," he said. "This is a great honor. Don't worry, he speaks perfect English."

I nodded, feeling a little nervous.

Jampa was standing at the door looking expectant.

"I am to escort you—now," he said.

I got up and followed as Jampa led me through a very large room with high ceilings and into a smaller room on the other side. Five or six monks, holding prayer wheels and white scarves, watched with anticipation as we walked up toward the front and sat down. Yin waved from the far corner.

"This is the greeting room," Jampa said.

The interior of the room was wooden and painted a light blue. Handcrafted murals and mandalas adorned the walls. We waited for a few minutes and then the Lama entered. He was taller than most of the other monks, but was dressed in a red robe, exactly like the ones they wore. After looking at everyone in the room very deliberately, he summoned Jampa forward. They touched foreheads, and he whispered something in Jampa's ear.

Jampa immediately turned and gestured to all the other

monks to follow him out of the room. Yin, too, began to leave, but as he did, he glanced at me and nodded slightly, a gesture I took as support for my impending conversation. Many of the monks handed me their scarves and nodded excitedly.

When the room was empty, the Lama motioned for me to come forward and sit in a tiny straight-back chair to his right. I bowed slightly as I came up and sat down.

"Thank you for seeing me," I said.

He nodded and smiled, looking me over for a long time.

"Could I ask you about my friend Wilson James?" I finally inquired. "Do you know where he is?"

"What is your understanding of Shambhala?" the Lama asked in return.

"I guess I've always thought of it as an imaginary place, a fantasy. You know, like Shangri-La."

He cocked his head and replied matter-of-factly, "It is a real place on Earth that exists as part of the human community."

"Why has no one ever discovered where it is? And why do so many prominent Buddhists speak of Shambhala as a way of life, a mentality?"

"Because Shambhala does represent a way of being and living. It can be spoken of accurately in that manner. But it is also an actual location where real people have achieved this way of being in community with each other."

"Have you been there?"

"No, no, I have not yet been called."

"Then how can you be so sure?"

"Because I have dreamed of Shambhala many times, as have many other adepts on the Earth. We compare our dreams and they are so similar we know this must be a real place. And we hold the sacred knowledge, the legends, that explain our relationship to this sacred community."

"What is that relationship?"

"We are to preserve the knowledge while we are waiting for the time when Shambhala will come out and make itself known to all peoples."

"Yin told me that some believe that the warriors of Shambhala will eventually arrive to defeat the Chinese."

"Yin's anger is very dangerous for him."

"He's wrong, then?"

"He is speaking from the human viewpoint that sees defeat in terms of war and physical fighting. Exactly how this prophecy will come true is still unknown. We will have to first understand Shambhala. But we know that this will be a different kind of battle."

I found the last statement cryptic, but his manner was so compassionate that I felt awe rather than confusion.

"We believe," Lama Rigden continued, "that the time when the way of Shambhala shall be known in the world is very close."

"Lama, how do you know this?"

"Again, because of our dreams. Your friend Wil has been here, as you undoubtedly have already heard. This we took as a great sign because we had earlier dreamed of him. He has smelled the fragrance and heard the utterance."

I was taken aback. "What kind of fragrance?"

He smiled. "The one you yourself smelled earlier today."

Now everything made sense. The way the monks had reacted and the Lama's decision to see me.

"You are also being called," he added. "The sending of the fragrance is a rare thing. I have seen it occur only twice—once when I was with my teacher, and again when your friend Wil was here. Now it has happened again with you. I had not known whether to see you or not. It is very dangerous to speak of these things trivially. Have you also heard the cry?"

"No," I said. "I don't understand what that is."

"It is also a call from Shambhala. Just keep listening for a special sound. When you hear it, you will know what it is."

"Lama, I'm not sure I want to go anywhere. It seems very dangerous here for me. The Chinese seem to know who I am. I think I want to go back to the United States as soon as possible. Can you just tell me where I might find Wil? Is he somewhere close?"

The Lama shook his head, looking very sad. "No, I'm afraid he has committed to go on."

I was silent, and for a long moment the Lama just looked at me.

"There is something else you must know," he said. "It is very clear from the dreams that without you, Wil could not survive this attempt. For him to succeed, you will have to be there as well."

A wave of fear ran through me, and I looked away. This was not what I wanted to hear.

"The legends say," the Lama went on, "that in Shambhala each generation has a certain destiny that is publicly known and talked about. The same is true in human cultures outside of Shambhala. Sometimes great strength and clarity can be gained by looking at the courage and intent of the generation that came before us."

I wondered where he was going with this.

"Is your father alive?" he asked.

I shook my head. "He died a couple of years ago."

"Did he serve in the great war of the 1940s?"

"Yes," I replied, "he did."

"Was he in the fighting?"

"Yes, during most of the war."

"Did he tell you of his most fearful situation?"

His question took me back to discussions with my father during my youth. I thought for a moment.

"Probably the landing in Normandy in 1944 at Omaha Beach."

"Ah, yes," the Lama said. "I've seen your American movies about this landing. Have you seen them?"

"Yes, I have," I said. "They moved me very much."

"They told of the soldiers' fear and courage," he went on.

"Yes."

"Do you think you could have done such things?"

"I don't know. I don't see how they did it."

"Perhaps it was easier for them because it was the calling for a whole generation. On some level they all sensed it: the ones who fought, the ones who made the arms, the ones who provided the food. They saved the world at the time of its greatest peril."

He waited as though he expected me to ask a question, but I just looked at him.

"The calling of your generation is different," he said. "You, too, must save the world. But you must do so in a different way. You must understand that inside you is a great power that can be cultivated and extended, a mental energy that has always been called prayer."

"So I've been told," I said. "But I guess I still don't know how to use it."

To this he smiled and stood up, looking at me with a twinkle in his eye.

"Yes," he said. "I know. But you will, you will."

* * *

I lay down on the cot in my room and thought about what the Lama had told me. He had ended the conversation abruptly, waving off my remaining questions.

"Go and rest now," he had said, calling in several monks by ringing a loud bell. "We will talk again tomorrow."

Later both Jampa and Yin had made me recount everything the Lama had said. But the truth was that the Lama had left me with more questions than answers. I still did not know where Wil had gone or what the call of Shambhala really meant. It all sounded fanciful and dangerous.

Yin and Jampa had refused to discuss any of these questions. We had spent the rest of the evening eating and looking out at the landscape before going to bed early. Now I found myself staring up at the ceiling, unable to sleep, thoughts whirling in my head.

I replayed my whole experience in Tibet in my mind several times and then finally drifted into a fitful sleep. I dreamed of running through the crowds of Lhasa, seeking sanctuary at one of the monasteries. The monks at the door took one look at me and shut the door. Soldiers pursued. I ran down dark lanes and alleyways without hope until, at the end of one street, I looked to my right and saw a lighted area similar to the ones I had seen before. As I moved closer, the light gradually disappeared, but ahead of me was a gate. The soldiers were coming around the corner behind me, and I dashed through the gate and found myself in an icy landscape . . .

I woke up with a start. Where was I? Slowly I recognized the room and got to my feet and walked to the window. Dawn was just breaking toward the east, and I tried to shake off the dream and go back to bed, an idea that proved to be totally fruitless. I was wide awake.

Pulling on a pair of pants and a jacket, I walked downstairs and outside to the courtyard by the vegetable gardens and sat down on an ornate metal bench. As I stared out toward the sunrise, I heard something behind me. Turning, I saw the figure of a man moving toward me from the monastery. It was Lama Rigden.

I stood up and he bowed deeply.

"You are up early," he said. "I hope you slept well."

"Yes," I said, watching him as he walked forward and sprinkled a handful of grain in the fountain pond for the fish. The water swirled as they consumed the food.

"What were your dreams?" he said without looking at me.

I told him about the chase and seeing the lighted area. He looked at me in amazement.

"Have you had this experience in your waking life as well?" he asked.

"Several times on this trip," I said. "Lama, what is going on?"

He smiled and sat on a bench opposite me. "You are being helped by the dakini."

"I don't understand. What are the dakini? Wil left Yin a note in which he referred to the dakini, but I'd never heard of them before that."

"They are from the spiritual world. They usually appear as females, but they can take any form they wish. In the West they are known as angels, but they are even more mysterious than most think. I'm afraid they are truly known only by those in Shambhala. The legends say that they move with the light of Shambhala."

He paused and looked at me deeply. "Have you decided whether to answer this call?"

"I wouldn't know how to proceed," I said.

"The legends will guide you. They say that the time for Shambhala to be known will be recognized because many people will begin to understand how those in Shambhala live, the truth behind the prayer-energy. Prayer is not a power that is realized only when we sit down and decide to pray in a particular situation. Prayer works at these times, of course, but prayer is also working at other times."

"You're talking about a constant prayer-field?"

"Yes. Everything we expect, good or bad, conscious or unconscious, we are helping to bring into being. Our prayer is an energy or power that emanates out from us in all directions. In most people, who think in ordinary ways, this power is very weak and contradictory. But in others, who seem to achieve a lot in life, and who are very creative and successful, this field of energy is strong, although it is still usually unconscious. Most of those in this group have a strong field because they grew up in an environment where they learned to expect success and more or less take it for granted. They had strong role models whom they emulated. But the legends say that soon all people will learn about this power and understand that our ability to use this energy can be strengthened and extended.

"I have told you this to explain how to answer the call of Shambhala. To find this holy place, you must systematically extend your energy until you emanate enough creative strength to go there. The procedure for doing this is set forth in the legends and involves three important steps. There is also a fourth step, but it is known in its completeness only to those in Shambhala. That is why finding Shambhala is so difficult. Even if one successfully extends one's energy though the first three steps, one must have help in order to actually find the way to Shambhala. The dakini must open the gateway."

"You called the dakini spiritual beings. Do you mean souls that are in the afterlife who are acting as guides for us?"

"No, the dakini are other beings who act to awaken and guard humans. They are not and never were human."

"And they are the same as angels?"

The Lama smiled. "They are what they are. One reality. Each religion has a different name for them, just as each religion has a different way of describing God and how humans should live. But in every religion the experience of God, the energy of love, is exactly the same. Each religion has its own history of this relationship and way of speaking about it, but there is only one divine source. It is the same with angels."

"So you aren't strictly Buddhist?"

"Our sect and the legends we hold have their roots in Buddhism, but we stand for the synthesis of all religions. We believe each has its truth that must be incorporated with all the others. It is possible to do this without losing the sovereignty or basic truth of one's own traditional way. I would also call myself a Christian, for instance, and a Jew or a Muslim. We believe those in Shambhala also work for an integration of all religious truth. They work for this in the same spirit that the Dalai Lama makes the Kalachakra initiations known to anyone who has a sincere heart."

I just looked at him, trying to take it all in.

"Don't try to understand everything now," the Lama said. "Just know that the integration of all religious truth is important if the force of prayer-energy is to grow large enough to resolve the dangers posed by those who fear. Also remember that the dakini are real."

"What makes them act to help us?" I asked.

The Lama took a deep breath, thinking deeply. The question seemed to be a point of frustration for him.

"I have worked my whole life to understand this question," he said finally, "but I must admit that I do not know. I think that it is the great secret of Shambhala and will not be understood until Shambhala is understood."

"But you think," I interjected, "that the dakini are helping me?"

"Yes," he said firmly. "And your friend Wil."

"What about Yin? How does he figure in all this?"

"Yin met your friend Wil at this monastery. Yin has also dreamed of you, but in a different context from myself or the other lamas. Yin was educated in England and is very familiar with Western ways. He is to be your guide, although he is very reluctant, as you have no doubt seen. This is only because he does not want to let anyone down. He will be your guide and take you as far as he can go."

He paused again and looked at me expectantly.

"And what about the Chinese government?" I asked. "What are they doing? Why are they so interested in what is happening?"

The Lama lowered his eyes. "I do not know. They seem to sense that something is happening with Shambhala. They have always tried to suppress Tibetan spirituality, but now they seem to have discovered our sect. You must be very careful. They fear us greatly."

I looked away for a moment, still thinking about the Chinese.

"Have you decided?" he asked.

"You mean whether to go?"

He smiled compassionately. "Yes."

"I don't know. I'm not sure I have the courage to risk losing everything."

The Lama just kept looking at me and nodded.

"You said some things about the challenge of my generation," I said. "I still don't understand this."

"World War II, as well as the cold war," the Lama began, "was the previous generation's challenge to face. The great advances in technology had placed massive weapons in the hands of nations.

In their nationalistic fervor, the forces of totalitarianism were attempting to conquer the democratic countries. This threat would have prevailed had not ordinary citizens fought and died in defense of freedom, ensuring the success of democracy in the world.

"But your task is different from that of your parents. The mission of your generation is different in its very nature from that of the World War II generation. They had to fight a particular tyranny with violence and arms. You must fight against the concepts of war and enemies altogether. But it takes just as much heroism. Do you understand? There was no way your parents could have done what they did, but they persevered. So must you. The forces of totalitarianism have not gone away; they are just not expressing themselves any longer through nations seeking empire. The forces of tyranny now are international and much more subtle, taking advantage of our dependence on technology and credit and a desire for convenience. Out of fear, they seek to centralize all technological growth into the hands of a few, so that their economic positions can be safeguarded and the future evolution of the world controlled.

"Opposing them with force is impossible. Democracy must be guarded now with the next step in freedom's evolution. We must use the power of our vision, and the expectations that flow out from us, as a constant prayer. This power is stronger than anyone now knows, and we must master it and begin to use it before it is too late. There are signs that something is changing in Shambhala. It is opening, shifting."

The Lama was looking at me with steely determination. "You must answer the call to Shambhala. It is the only way to honor what your forefathers have done before you."

His comment filled me with anxiety.

"What do I do first?" I asked.

"Complete the extensions of your energy," the Lama replied. "This will not be easy for you because of your fear and anger. But if you persist, the gateway will present itself to you."

"The gateway?"

"Yes. Our legends say that there are several gateways into Shambhala: one in the eastern Himalayas in India, one to the northwest on the border of China, and one in the far north in Russia. The signs will guide you to the right one. When all seems lost, look for the dakini."

As the Lama was talking, Yin walked outside with our packs.

"Okay," I said, feeling increasingly terrified. "I'll try." Even as I spoke, I couldn't believe the words were coming from my mouth.

"Don't worry," Lama Rigden said. "Yin will help you. Just remember that before you can find Shambhala, you must first extend the level of energy that emanates from you and goes out into the world. You can't have success until you do. You must master the force of your expectations."

I looked at Yin and he half smiled.

"It's time," he said.

3

CULTIVATING ENERGY

We walked outside, and I noticed a brown, hardtop Jeep, perhaps ten years old, sitting beside the road. As we walked closer, I could tell it was filled with ice chests, boxes of dried food, sleeping bags, and heavier jackets. Several external gas tanks were strapped to the rear.

"Where did all this stuff come from?" I asked.

He winked at me. "We have been preparing for this journey for a long time."

From Lama Rigden's monastery, Yin headed north for a few miles and then turned the Jeep from the wide gravel road onto a narrow tract, barely wider than a foot path. We continued driving for several miles without saying anything.

The truth was, I didn't know what to say. I had agreed to go on this journey purely because of the Lama's words and because of what Wil had done for me in the past, but now the angst over the decision was beginning to set in. I tried to shake off the fear and to retrace in my mind all that Lama Rigden had told me. What did he mean by mastering the force of my expectations?

I looked over at Yin. He was staring intently at the road.

"Where are we heading?" I asked.

Without looking at me, he said, "This is a shortcut to the Friendship Highway. We must go southwest to Tingri, near Mount Everest. The drive will take most of the day. We will also be going up in altitude."

"Is that area safe?"

Yin glanced at me. "We will be very careful. We're going to find Mr. Hanh."

"Who is he?"

"He knows the most about the First Extension of prayer-energy you must learn. He is from Thailand, and he is very educated."

I shook my head and looked away. "I'm not sure I understand these extensions. What are they?"

"You know that you have an energy field, correct? A prayer-field flowing out from you all the time."

"Yes."

"And you know that this field has an effect on the world, on what happens? You know it can be either small and weak or extensive and strong."

"Yes, I suppose."

"Well, there are precise ways to extend and expand your field so that you can become more creative and powerful. The legends say that eventually all humans will know how to do this. But you must do it now if you expect to get to Shambhala and find Wil."

"Can you already perform these extensions?" I asked.

Yin frowned. "I did not say that."

I just looked at him. This was great. How was I supposed to learn to do this if even Yin had trouble?

For hours we drove without talking, eating nuts and vegetables as we rode along, stopping only once at a truck stop for gas. Well after dark, we passed through Tingri.

"We must be very careful here," Yin said. "We are near the Rongphu monastery and the Everest base camp, and there will be Chinese soldiers observing the tourists and climbers. But we will also be able to see incredible views of the north face of Everest."

Yin made several turns until he came to an area of old wooden buildings. Beyond them was a simple mud-brick house.

The yard around Hanh's dwelling was immaculate, with carefully planted beds and rock gardens. As we drove up, a large man in a colorful, hand-embroidered robe walked out on the stoop. He appeared to be in his sixties, but he moved like a person much younger. His head was completely shaved.

Yin waved as the man strained to see who it was. When he recognized Yin, he burst into a smile and walked toward us as we got out of the Jeep.

The two men spoke for a moment in Tibetan, then Yin pointed to me and said, "This is my American friend."

I told Hanh my name, and he bowed slightly and grasped my hand.

"Welcome," he said. "Please come in."

As Hanh walked back to the house, Yin reached inside the Jeep and grabbed his pack. "Bring your satchel," he said.

The house inside was modest but filled with colorful Tibetan paintings and rugs. We went into a small sitting area, and from where I was I could see most of the other rooms. To the left was a small kitchen and a bedroom, and to the right was another room that had the look of a treatment area of some kind. In the center of the room was a massage or examination table, and lining one wall were cabinets and a small sink.

Yin said something else to Hanh in Tibetan, and I heard him repeat my name. Hanh leaned forward with a new alertness. He glanced over at me and took a large breath.

"You are very fearful," Hanh said, looking me over closely.

"No kidding," I replied.

Hanh chuckled at my sarcasm. "We must do something about that if you are going to complete your journey."

He walked around me, surveying my body.

"Those in Shambhala," he began, "live differently from most other humans. They always have. In fact, through the millennia, there has been a great gulf between the energy levels of most people and those in Shambhala. Yet in recent times, as all humans have evolved and increased their consciousness, this distance has closed, but it is still very far apart."

As Hanh was talking, I glanced at Yin. He seemed to be as nervous as I was.

Hanh picked up on it too. "Yin is as fearful as you are," he said. "But he knows that this fear can be handled. I don't think you realize that yet. You must begin to act and think as those in Shambhala do. You must first cultivate and then stabilize your energy."

Hanh stopped and concentrated on looking at my body again, then smiled.

"You have had many experiences," he said. "You should be stronger."

"Maybe I don't understand energy well enough," I replied.

"Oh no, you understand." Hanh smiled broadly. "You just don't want to change the way you live. You want to get excited about the ideas and then live unconsciously, more or less the way you've always done."

This conversation was not going the way I wanted, and my fear was being replaced by a mild irritation.

As I stood there, Hanh walked around me several more times, still gazing intently up and down my body.

"What are you looking at?" I asked.

"When I am assessing someone's energy level, I first look at posture," Hanh said matter-of-factly. "Yours is not too bad at this point, but you had to work on it, didn't you?"

His question was very perceptive. As a youth, I grew very quickly one year and as a result slumped terribly. My back was always tired and ached, and it only improved when I began to practice a few basic yoga positions every morning.

"The energy still doesn't flow up your body very well," Hanh added.

"You can tell that by looking at me?" I responded.

"And by feeling you. The amount and strength of your energy feels like the degree of presence you have in the room. Surely you must have experienced someone who came into a room and had presence or charisma."

"Sure, of course." I thought again about the man at the hotel pool in Kathmandu.

"The more energy one has, the more others feel that person's presence. Often this is energy that winds up being displayed through the ego, and so feels strong at first, then dissipates very rapidly. But with others, this is a genuine and constant energy that remains reliable."

I nodded.

"One thing in your favor is that you are open," Hanh continued. "You have experienced a mystical opening, a sudden inflow of divine energy, sometime in the past, have you not?"

"Yes," I said, remembering my experience on the mountaintop in Peru. Even now it remained vivid in my memory. I had been at the end of my rope, certain I was about to be killed by Peruvian soldiers, when all of a sudden I was imbued with an unusual calm, euphoria, and lightness. It was the first time I had experienced what the mystics of various religions have called a transformative state.

"How did the energy fill you?" Hanh asked. "How did it happen exactly?"

"It was a rush of peacefulness, and all my fear went away."

"How did it move?"

That was a question I had never thought about, but I quickly began to remember. "It seemed to come up my spine and out through the top of my head, lifting my body upward. I felt as if I was floating. As though there was a string pulling me upward from the top of my head."

Hanh nodded approvingly, then caught my eye. "And how long did it last?"

"Not long," I replied. "But I have learned how to breathe in the beauty around me in order to rekindle the feeling."

"What is missing in your practice," said Hanh, "is breathing in the energy and then consciously maintaining it at a higher level. This is the first extension that you must make. You must keep your energy flowing in more fully. This must be done in a precise manner, taking care that your other actions do not erode your energy field once you have built it up."

He paused for a moment. "Do you understand? The rest of your life must support your higher energy. You must be congruent." He glanced at me mischievously. "You must live wisely. Let's eat."

He disappeared into the kitchen, and returned with a platter of vegetables, accompanied by a sauce of some kind. He ushered both Yin and me over to a table and served the vegetables in three small bowls. It soon became clear that the food was all part of the information Hanh was imparting.

As we ate, he continued. "Maintaining higher energy within oneself is impossible if one consumes dead matter as food."

I looked away, turning off. If this was going to be a lecture on diet, I would just as soon skip it.

My attitude seemed to infuriate Hanh.

"Are you crazy?" he almost shouted. "Your very survival may depend on this information and you won't put yourself out a little bit to learn this. What do you think? That you can live any way you want and still do important things?"

He became quiet and glanced sideways at me. I realized that the anger was genuine but was also part of his act. I got the impression that he was giving information to me on more than one level. As I looked back at him, I couldn't help smiling. Hanh was eminently likable.

He patted my shoulder and smiled back at me.

"Most people," he continued, "are full of energy and enthusiasm in their youth, but then during middle age they lapse into a slow, downhill slide that they pretend not to notice. After all, their friends are slowing down and their kids are active, so they spend more and more time sitting around and eating the foods that taste good.

"Before long, they begin to have nagging complaints and chronic problems such as digestive difficulties or skin irritations that they write off as just age, and then one day they get a serious illness that won't go away. Usually they go to a doctor who does not stress prevention and they begin to take drugs, and sometimes the problem is helped and sometimes it isn't. And then, as the years fly by, they get some disease that progressively gets worse, and they realize they are dying. Their only solace is that they think what is happening occurs to everyone—that it is inevitable.

"The terrible thing is that this collapse of energy happens to some extent even to people who otherwise intend to be spiritual." He leaned over toward me and feigned looking around the room to see if someone was listening. "This includes some of our most respected lamas."

I wanted to laugh but I dared not.

"If we seek higher energy and at the same time consume foods that rob us of this energy," Hanh continued, "we get nowhere. We must assess all the energies we routinely allow into our own energy fields, especially foods, and avoid all but the best if our fields are to stay strong."

He leaned closer to me again. "This is very difficult for most people because we are all addicted to the foods we currently eat, and most are horribly poisonous."

I looked away.

"I know there is much conflicting information out there about food," he went on. "But the truth is out there too. Each of us must do the research, make ourselves see the larger picture. We are spiritual beings who come into this world to raise our energy. Yet much of what we find here is designed purely for sensual pleasure and distraction, and much of it saps our energy and pulls us toward physical disintegration. If we really believe we are energetic beings, we must follow a narrow path through these temptations.

"If you look all the way back at evolution, you see that from the beginning we had to experiment with food purely by trial and error, just to figure out which foods were good for us and which would kill us. Eat this plant, survive; eat that one over there, die. At this point in history we've figured out what kills us, but we're only now realizing which foods add to our ultimate longevity and keep our energy high, and which ones ultimately wear us down."

He paused for a moment as if determining whether I was understanding.

"In Shambhala they see this larger picture," he continued. "They know who we are as human beings. We look like we are material stuff, flesh and blood, but we are atoms! Pure energy!

Your science has proved this fact. When we look deeper into atoms, we first see particles, and then, at deeper levels, the particles themselves disappear into patterns of pure energy, vibrating at a certain level. And if we look at the way we eat from this perspective, we see that what we put in our bodies as food affects our vibrational state. Certain foods increase our energy and vibration and others diminish it. The truth is as simple as that.

"All disease is the result of a drop in vibrational energy, and when our energy drops to a certain point, there are natural forces in the world that are designed to disincorporate our bodies."

He looked at me as though he had said something very profound.

"Do you mean physically disincorporate?" I asked.

"Yes. Look again at the larger picture. When anything dies—a dog hit by a car, or a person after a long illness—the cells of the body immediately lose their vibration and become very acid in chemistry. That acid state is the signal to the microbes of the world, the viruses, bacteria, and fungi, that it is time to decompose this dead tissue. This is their job in the physical universe. To return a body back to the earth.

"I said earlier," he went on, "that when our bodies drop in energy because of the kinds of foods we are eating, it makes us susceptible to disease. Here's how that works. When we eat foods, they are metabolized and leave a waste or ash in our bodies. This ash is either acidic in nature or alkaline, depending on the food. If it is alkaline, then it can be quickly extracted from our bodies with little energy. However, if these waste products are acid, they are very hard for the blood and lymph system to eliminate and they are stored in our organs and tissues as solids—low vibrational crystalline forms that create blocks or disruptions in the vibratory levels of our cells. The more such acid by-products are stored, the more generally acid these tissues become, and guess what?"

He looked at me dramatically again. "A microbe of one type or another appears and senses all this acid and says, 'Oh, this body is ready to be decomposed.'

"Do you get that? When any organism dies, its body quickly changes to a highly acid environment and is consumed by microbes very quickly. If we begin to resemble this very acid, or death state, then we begin to come under attack from microbes. All human diseases are the result of such an attack."

What Hanh was saying made perfect sense. A long time ago, I had run across some information about body pH on the Internet. Moreover, I seemed to know it intuitively.

"You're telling me that what we eat directly sets us up for disease?" I asked.

"Yes, the wrong foods can lower our vibrational level to the point that the forces of nature begin to return our bodies to the earth."

"What about diseases that aren't caused by microbes?"

"All disease comes about through microbial action. Your own research in the West is showing that. Various microbes have been found to be associated with the arterial lesions of heart disease, as well as the production of tumors in cancer. But remember, the microbes are just doing what they do. Diets that create the acidic environment are the true cause."

He paused and then said, "Grasp this fully. We humans are either in an alkaline, high energy state or we are in an acid state, which signals the microbes living within us, or that come by, that we are ready to decompose. Disease is literally a rotting of some part of our bodies because the microbes around us have been given the signal that we are already dead."

He looked at me mischievously again.

"Sorry to be so blunt," he said. "But we don't have much time. The food we eat determines almost entirely which of these two conditions we are in. Generally, foods that leave acid wastes in our body are heavy, overcooked, overprocessed, and sweet, such as meats, flours, pastries, alcohol, coffee, and the sweeter fruits. Alkaline foods are greener, fresher, and more alive, such as fresh vegetables and their juices, leafy greens, sprouts, and fruits like avocado, tomato, grapefruit, and lemons. It could not be more simple. We are spiritual beings in an energetic, spiritual world. Those of you in the West might have grown up thinking that cooked meat and processed foods are good for us. But we know now that they create an environment of slow disincorporation that takes its toll on us over time.

"All the debilitating illnesses that plague mankind—arteriosclerosis, stroke, arthritis, AIDS, and especially cancers—exist because we pollute our bodies, which signals the microbes inside that we are ready to break down, deenergize, die. We always wondered why some people exposed to the same microbes don't get a particular disease. The difference is the inner-body environment. The good news is that even if we have too much acidity in our bodies and begin to decompose, the situation can be reversed if we improve our nutrition and move to an alkaline, higher energy state."

He was now waving both arms, his eyes wide, still twinkling.

"We are living in the dark ages when it comes to the principles of a vibrant, high-energy body. Human beings are supposed to live more than a hundred and fifty years. But we eat in a way that immediately begins to destroy us. Everywhere, we see people who are disincorporating before our eyes. But it doesn't have to be that way."

He paused and took a breath. "It's not that way in Shambhala."

After another moment Hanh began to walk around, looking me over one more time.

"So, there you have it," he concluded. "The legends say that humans will first learn the true nature of foods and what kinds to consume. Then, the legends say, we can fully open up to the inner sources of energy that increase our vibration even more."

He slid his chair back from the table and looked at me. "You are handling the altitude very well here in Tibet, but I would like for you to rest."

"That would be nice," I said. "I'm bushed."

"Yes," Yin agreed, "we have had a long day."

"Make sure you expect a dream," Hanh added, leading me toward a bedroom.

"Expect a dream?"

Hanh turned. "Yes, you are more powerful than you think."

I laughed.

I woke up suddenly and looked out the window. The sun was well up in the sky. No dream. I put on my shoes and walked into the other room.

Hanh and Yin were sitting at the table, talking.

"How did you sleep?" Hanh asked.

"Okay," I said, slumping down in one of the chairs. "But I can't remember dreaming."

"That's because you don't have enough energy," he said, half-distracted. He was staring intensely at my body again. I realized he was focused on the way I was sitting.

"What are you looking at?" I asked.

"Is this the way you wake up in the morning?" Hanh inquired.

I stood up. "What's wrong?"

"After sleep, one must wake up one's body and begin to accept the energy before one does anything else." He was standing with his legs far apart and his hands on his hips. As I watched, he slid his feet together and lifted his arms. His body rose up in one motion until he was standing on his tiptoes with his palms pressed together directly over his head.

I blinked. There was something unusual about the way his body moved, and I couldn't focus on it exactly. He seemed to float upward rather than use his muscles. When I could focus again, he was beaming a broad smile. Just as quickly, his body moved from there into a graceful walk toward me. I blinked again.

"Most people wake up slowly," Hanh said, "and slouch around and get themselves going with a cup of coffee or tea. They go to a job in which they continue to slouch around or use just one particular set of muscles. Patterns set in, and as I said, blocks develop in the way energy flows through our bodies.

"You must make sure your body is open everywhere in order to receive all the energy that is available. You do this by moving every muscle, every morning, from your center." He pointed to a place just below his navel. "If you concentrate on moving from this area, then your muscles will be free to operate at their highest level of coordination. It is the central principle of all the martial arts and dance disciplines. You can even invent your own movements."

With this comment, he launched into a multitude of movements I had never seen before. It appeared to be something like the shifts of weight and the twirling that one sees in tai chi. He was definitely performing an expansion of these classical movements.

"Your body," he added, "will know how to move in order to help loosen your individual blocks."

He stood on one leg and leaned over and swung his arm as if he were pitching a softball underhanded, only his hand almost touched the floor as he made the movement. Then he spun around in place on the opposite leg. I never saw his weight shift, and again he seemed to be floating.

I shook my head and tried to focus, but he had stopped in place, as if a photographer had frozen his movements in a snapshot, which appeared impossible. Just as suddenly he was walking toward me again.

"How do you do this?" I asked.

He said, "I began slowly and remembered the basic principle. If you move from your center and expect the energy to flow into you, you will move in a lighter and lighter manner. Of course, to perfect this you must be able to open up to all the divine energy that is available within."

He stopped and looked at me. "How well do you remember your mystical opening?"

I thought again about Peru and my experience on the mountaintop.

"Fairly well, I think."

"This is good," he said. "Let's go outside."

Yin smiled as he got up, and we followed Hanh out into a small garden and up some steps into an area of sparse brown grass and large, jagged boulders. The rocks had attractive streaks of reds and browns running through them. For ten minutes Hanh led me through some of the movements I had seen earlier, then offered me a place to sit down on the ground, taking a seat to my right. Yin sat down behind us. The morning sun bathed the mountains in the distance in a warm yellow light. I was struck by their beauty.

"The legends say," Hanh began, "that opening up to a higher energy state is an ability that all humans will eventually acquire. It will begin as a general knowledge that such an awareness is possible. Then we will move to an understanding of all the factors involved in cultivating and maintaining higher levels of energy."

He paused and looked at me. "You already know the basic procedure, but your senses must be expanded. The legends say that first you calm yourself and look out on your surroundings. Most of us seldom look closely at the things around us. It's just stuff that takes a backseat to whatever is on our minds to get done. But we must remember that everything in the universe is alive with spiritual energy and is a part of God. We must intentionally ask to connect with the divine inside us.

"As you know, the measure as to whether we are connecting with this energy is our sense of beauty. Always ask yourself this question: How beautiful does everything look? No matter how it appears at first we can always see more beauty in it if we try. The degree of beauty we can see measures how much divine energy we are receiving within us."

Hanh went on to have me spend some time looking, really looking, at everything around me.

"Once we begin to establish our connection," he said, "and experience the divine energy within, everything begins to have more presence in our perception. Things stand out and we notice their unique shape and color. When this perception occurs, we can breathe in even more energy.

"You see, in reality, the energy doesn't come so much from the things around us—although we can absorb energy directly from some plants and sacred sites. Sacred energy comes from our connection to the divine inside us. Everything around us, both natural and man-made—flowers, rocks, grass, mountains, art—is already majestically beautiful and present beyond anything most humans can perceive. All we do, when we open up to the divine, is raise our energy vibration and thus our perceptual ability so we can view the world the way it already is. Do you understand?

Humans already live in a world of immense beauty and color and form. Heaven itself is right here. We just haven't opened up to enough inner energy to see it."

I listened with fascination. This was clearer now than ever before.

"Focus on the beauty," Hanh instructed, "and begin to breathe in the energy within you."

I took a deep breath.

"Now look for increases in the beauty as you breathe," Hanh instructed.

I gazed out again at the rocks and mountains, and to my amazement I noticed that the tallest of the ridges in the distance was Mount Everest. For some reason, I hadn't recognized its shape before.

"Yes, yes, look at Everest," Hanh said.

As I gazed out at the mountain, I noticed that the snow-rippled ridges on its face seemed to make little steps up toward the crown-shaped peak. The sight jolted my perception outward, and the world's tallest mountain instantly seemed closer, somehow part of me, as if I might be able to reach out and touch it.

"Keep breathing," Hanh said. "Your vibration and ability to perceive will increase even more. Everything will become shiny, as though illuminated from within."

I took another breath and I began to feel lighter and my back straightened with little effort. Unbelievably I felt exactly as I had during the mountain experience in Peru.

Hanh was nodding. "Your ability to perceive beauty is the primary measure that divine energy is coming into you. But there are other measures as well.

"You will feel lighter," Hanh continued. "The energy will rise up through you and lift you up, as you said, like a string pulling you up from the top of your head. And you will feel a greater wisdom about who you are and what you are doing. You will receive intuitions and dreams about what is next on your life path."

He paused and looked at my body. I was now sitting up effortlessly. "Now we come to the most important part," he said. "You must learn to sustain this energy, to keep it flowing into you. You must use the power of your expectations here, the power of your prayer-energy."

Here was this word again: *expectation.* I had never heard it used in this context before.

"How do I do that?" I asked, feeling confused, my body dropping in energy, the forms and colors around me fading.

Hanh's eyes got large and he burst into laughter. He tried several times to stop but finally rolled on the ground in uncontrollable mirth. He regained his composure several times but began laughing again every time he looked at me. I even heard Yin snickering in the background.

Finally Hanh managed to take some breaths and calm down.

"I'm very sorry," he said. "It's just that your expression was so funny. You really don't believe you have any power at all, do you?"

"It's not that," I protested. "I just don't know what you meant by expectation."

Hanh was still smiling. "You do think you carry around certain expectations about life, don't you? You expect the sun to rise. You expect your blood to circulate."

"Of course."

"Well, I'm only asking that you try to become conscious of these expectations. It is the only way to maintain and extend the higher level of energy that you just experienced. You must learn to expect that level of energy in your life, and you must do so very deliberately and consciously. This is the only way to complete the first prayer extension. Would you like to try again?"

I smiled back at him, and we spent several minutes breathing and building up the energy. When I was seeing the higher level of beauty I had experienced before, I nodded at him.

"Now," he said, "you must expect this energy that is filling you to keep filling you and to flow out of you in every direction. Visualize this happening."

I tried to hold on to my energy level as I asked, "This out-flow—how do I know this is really happening?"

"You will be able to feel it. Just visualize it for now."

I took another breath and visualized the energy coming into me and flowing out in every direction into the world.

"I still don't know whether it's really happening," I said.

Hanh looked directly at me, appearing slightly impatient. "You know the energy is flowing out of you because the energy is maintained, the colors and shapes stay high, and you feel it as it fills you, then overflows outward."

"How does it feel?" I asked.

He looked at me with incredulity. "You know the answer to that."

I gazed out at the mountains again, visualizing the energy flow going out of me toward them. They remained beautiful and began to be immensely attractive as well. Then a rush of deep emotion filled me, and I remembered what I had experienced in Peru.

Hanh was nodding.

"Of course!" I said. "The measure of whether the energy is flowing out is the feeling of love."

Hanh smiled broadly. "Yes, it is a love that becomes a background emotion that stays with you as long as your prayer-energy is going out into the world. You must stay in a state of love."

"This seems awfully idealistic for ordinary human beings," I said.

Hanh chuckled. "I'm not telling you how to be an ordinary human being. I'm telling you how to be at the edge of evolution. I'm telling you how to be a hero. Just remember that you must expect divine energy to come into you at a higher level and to flow out of you like a cup running over. When you get disconnected, remember this feeling of love. Try to consciously rekindle the state."

His eyes twinkled again. "Your expectation is the key to whether you can maintain this experience. You must visualize it happening, believe that it will be there for you in all situations. This expectation must be cultivated and consciously affirmed every day."

I nodded.

"Now," he said, "do you understand all the procedures I have told you about?"

Before I could answer, he said, "The key is how you wake up in the morning. That is why I asked you to sleep, so that I could see how you wake up. You must do so with discipline. Wake your body up to the inflow of energy in the manner that I showed you. Move from your center, feel the energy immediately. Expect it immediately.

"Eat only the foods that are still alive, and after a while, inner divine energy will be easier to breathe into your being. Take the time to fill up with energy every day and wake up with movement. Remember the measures. Visualize that this energy is coming into you and feel it as if flows out into the world. Do this and you will have completed the First Extension. You will be able not just to experience energy occasionally, but to cultivate it and maintain it at a higher level."

He bowed low and without saying anything else walked back toward the house. Yin and I followed. When we arrived, Hanh began selecting food and placing it in a large basket.

"What about the gateway?" I asked Hanh.

He stopped and looked at me. "There are many gateways."

"I mean, do you know where we can find the gateway to Shambhala?"

He looked at me sternly. "You have only completed one extension of your prayer-energy. You now must learn what to do with this energy that is flowing out of you. And you are very headstrong, and still prone to fear and anger. You will have to overcome these tendencies before you can get anywhere near Shambhala."

With that statement, Hanh nodded at Yin and handed him the basket, then walked into the other room.

4

CONSCIOUS ALERTNESS

I walked out to the Jeep, feeling incredibly good. The air was cool and the mountains in every direction still seemed luminous. We got in the vehicle, and Yin pulled away.

"Do you know where to go now?" I asked.

"I know that we must head toward northwest Tibet. According to the legends, that is the closest gateway to us. But, as Lama Rigden said, we will have to be shown."

Yin paused and glanced at me. "It is time that I told you about my dream."

"The dream that Lama Rigden mentioned?" I asked. "The one you had of me?"

"Yes, in this dream we are together journeying across Tibet, looking for the gateway. And we could not find it. We journeyed very far and traveled in circles, lost. But at the moment of our greatest despair, we met someone who knew where we should go."

"What happened after that?"

"The dream ended."

"Who was the person? Was it Wil?"

"No, I don't think so."

"What do you think the dream means?"

"It means we must be very alert."

We rode in silence for a few moments and then I asked, "Are there many soldiers stationed in northwest Tibet?"

"Not usually," he replied. "Except on the border or at the military bases. The problem is getting through the next three or four hundred miles, past Mount Kailash and Lake Manasarovar. There are several military checkpoints."

For four hours we rode without incident, traveling for a while on graded gravel roads and then turning onto various dirt tracts for a time. We reached Saga without any difficulty and hit what Yin told me was the southern route into western Tibet. We passed mostly large transport trucks or local Tibetans in older cars or in carts. A few foreign hitchhikers could be seen around the truck stops.

After another hour Yin pulled the Jeep off the main road and onto what amounted to only a horse path. The Jeep bounced over deep gullies.

"There is usually a Chinese checkpoint up ahead on the main road," Yin said. "We must go around."

We were traveling up a steep slope, and when we got to the crest of the hill, Yin stopped the Jeep and led me to the edge of a cliff. Below us, several hundred feet away we could see two large military trucks with Chinese insignia. Perhaps a dozen soldiers were standing by the road.

"This is not good," Yin said. "There are usually only a few soldiers at this crossroads. They may still be looking for us."

I tried to shake off a rush of anxiety and keep my energy high. I thought I saw several of the soldiers looking up the hill toward us, so I ducked down.

"Something is happening," Yin whispered.

When I looked back at the crossroads, the soldiers were searching a van that had driven into the checkpoint. A middle-aged blond man was standing on the side of the road being interrogated. Someone else was still in the van. We could just barely hear a European language being spoken, sounding very much like Dutch.

"Why are they being detained?" I asked Yin.

"I don't know," he said. "They may not have the correct permits, or perhaps they asked the wrong questions."

I lingered, wishing I could help.

"Please," Yin said. "We must go."

We got in the Jeep, and Yin drove slowly around the rest of the hill and down the slope on the other side. At the bottom we hit another narrow track that turned to the right, away from the crossroads, still heading northwest. We traveled on this road for about five more miles, before it merged back into the main road and into Zhongba, a small town with several hotels and a few shops. Here there were people walking, leading yaks and other livestock, and several land cruisers drove by.

"We are now just one of the pilgrims heading to Mount Kailash," Yin said. "We will be less noticeable."

I wasn't convinced. In fact, half a mile farther a Chinese military truck pulled onto the road directly behind us, and another surge of fear ran through me. Yin turned onto a side street and the truck moved past us and out of sight.

"You must stay strong," Yin said. "It is time for you to learn the Second Extension."

He went on to guide me through the First Extension again until I could visualize and feel my energy flowing out in front of us and into the distance.

"Now that you have your energy moving out, you must set this field of energy to have a certain effect."

His comment fascinated me. "Set my field?"

"Yes. We can direct our prayer-field to act on the world in various ways. We do this by using our expectations. You have already done this once, remember? Hanh taught you to expect that the energy would keep flowing through you. Now you must set your field with other expectations and do so with true discipline. Otherwise, all your energy can quickly collapse in fear and anger."

He looked at me with a sad expression I had never seen before.

"What's wrong?" I asked.

"When I was young, I watched a Chinese soldier kill my father. I hate and fear them intensely. And I must confess something: I myself am part Chinese. This is the worst part. It is this memory and guilt that erodes my energy, so that I tend to anticipate the worst. You will learn that at these higher levels of energy, our fields of prayer act very quickly to bring to us exactly what we expect. If we fear, it brings to us what we fear. If we hate, it brings us more of what we hate.

"Thankfully when we go into these negative expectations, our prayer-fields collapse rather quickly because we lose our connection with the divine and are no longer outflowing love. But a fear expectation can still be powerful. That is why you must monitor your expectations carefully and set your field consciously."

He smiled at me and added, "Because you don't hate the Chinese military the way I do, you have an advantage. But you still have much fear, and you seem to be capable of great anger . . . just like me. Perhaps that is why we are together."

I was looking ahead at the road as we drove, thinking about what Yin was saying, not believing that our thoughts could be that powerful. My reverie was interrupted when Yin slowed the Jeep and parked in front of a line of dusty frame buildings.

"Why are you stopping?" I asked. "Won't we draw more attention to ourselves this way?"

"Yes," he said. "But we must risk it. The soldiers have spies everywhere, but we have no choice. It is not safe to go into the western areas of Tibet with only one vehicle. There are no places to make repairs. We must find someone to go with us."

"What if they turn us in?"

Yin looked at me in horror. "That won't happen if we get the right people. Watch your thoughts. I told you we have to set the right field around us. It is important."

He started to get out of the car but hesitated. "You must do better than me in this regard or we have no chance. Focus on setting your field for *rten brel*."

I was silent for a moment. "*Rten brel?* What's that?"

"It is the Tibetan word for synchronicity. You must set your field to stay in the synchronistic process, to bring the intuitions, the coincidences, to help us."

Yin glanced at the building and got out of the Jeep, indicating with his hand that he wanted me to stay.

For almost an hour I waited, watching the Tibetan people walk by. Occasionally I would see someone who looked Indian or European. At one point I even thought I saw the Dutchman we had seen at the checkpoint pass on a distant street. I strained to see, but I couldn't be sure.

Where was Yin? I wondered. The last thing I needed was to be separated again. I imagined myself driving through this town all alone, lost, having no idea where to go. What would I do?

Finally I saw Yin leave the building. For a moment he hesitated, looking both ways carefully before walking to the Jeep.

"I found two people I know," he said as he climbed behind the wheel. "I think they will do." He was trying to be convincing, but his tone of voice betrayed his doubt.

He started up the car and we drove on. Five minutes later we passed a small restaurant made entirely from corrugated tin. Yin parked the Jeep about two hundred feet from the restaurant, hiding it behind some oil storage tanks. We were on the outskirts of town now and almost no one was on the street. Inside the building, we found one room with six rickety tables. A narrow, whitewashed bar separated us from the kitchen, where several women worked. One of the women saw us sit down and came over to us.

Yin spoke briefly to her in Tibetan, and I caught the word for soup. The woman nodded and looked at me.

"The same," I said to Yin, taking off my coat and draping it behind me on the chair. "And water." Yin translated and the woman smiled and walked away.

Yin turned serious. "Did you understand what I said earlier? You must now set a field that brings more synchronicity."

I nodded. "How do I set that field?"

"The first thing you must do is make sure you build on the First Extension. Be certain the energy is flowing into you and out into the world. Feel the measures. Set your expectation for this energy to be constant. Now you must expect that your prayer-field will act to bring forth just the thoughts and events necessary for your best destiny to unfold. In order to set this field around you, you must keep yourself in a state of conscious alertness."

"Alert for what?"

"For synchronicity. You must keep yourself in a state where you are constantly looking for the next mysterious bit of information that helps you toward your destiny. Some synchronicity will come to you no matter what you do, but you can increase the occurrence if you set a constant field by always expecting it."

I reached into my back pants pocket for my notebook. Although I hadn't used it before, I had an intuition to make note of what Yin was saying. Then I remembered that I had left the notebook in the Jeep.

"It's locked," he said, handing me the keys with a nod of his head. "Don't go anywhere else."

I went straight to the Jeep and retrieved the notebook and was about to head back when the sound of vehicles pulling up to the restaurant startled me. I moved back behind the tanks and looked out at the scene. In front of the restaurant were two gray, Chinese-built trucks. Five or six men in plain clothes got out of the trucks and went into the restaurant. From where I was, I could see inside through the windows. The men lined everyone up against the walls and began to search them. I tried to locate Yin but couldn't see him anywhere. Did he escape?

A new land cruiser pulled up outside, and a tall, lanky Chinese official in a military uniform got out and walked toward the door. He was clearly the man in charge. At the door he looked inside briefly, then stopped and turned around, looking up both sides of the street, as though sensing something. He turned my way and I ducked behind the bins again, my heart racing.

After a moment I risked a glance toward the restaurant. The Chinese were bringing out the people and loading them into the trucks. Yin wasn't among them. One of the cars drove away as the officer in charge spoke to the remaining men. He seemed to be directing them to search the street.

I ducked around the tanks and took a large breath. I knew if I stayed there, it would be only a matter of time before they found me. Looking for options, I noticed a narrow dirt alleyway that ran from the tanks through to the next street. I jumped into the Jeep, put it into neutral, and used the small incline of the street to roll through the alley, turning right on the next corner. I started the vehicle but had no idea where I was going. All I wanted to do was put some distance between me and the soldiers.

After a few blocks, I took a left onto a narrow lane which took me into an area that had few buildings. A hundred more yards and I seemed to be completely out of town. A mile later I pulled off the road and parked behind a cluster of high rocky mounds each the size of a house.

Now what? I thought. I was completely lost, with absolutely no idea where to go. A flash of anger and frustration raced through me. Yin should have prepared me for this possibility. Probably someone he knew in town could help me, but I had no way to find anyone now.

A flock of crows landed on the mound to my right, then flew up over the Jeep and circled, cawing loudly. I looked out the windows in both directions, certain that someone was disturbing the birds, but I saw no one. After a few minutes most of the crows flew toward the west, still cawing. But one stayed at the top of the mound, silently looking in my direction. That's good, I thought. He can be a sentry. I could stay put until I decided what to do.

In the back of the Jeep, I found some dried fruit and nuts, along with some crackers. I ate them unconsciously, taking occasional nervous drinks from the canteen of water. I knew I had to devise a plan. It came to me to head further up the road to the west, but I decided against it. A great fear was overwhelming me now, and I wanted only what I had desired all along: to forget about this trek and get back to Lhasa and then to the airport. I knew I could remember some of the turns, but the others I would have to guess at. I couldn't believe I hadn't tried to call someone at Lama Rigden's monastery or later at Hanh's, to set up an escape plan.

As I thought about what to do, my heart froze. I could hear the first rumblings of a vehicle coming down the road in my direction. I thought about starting the Jeep and pulling away but realized the vehicle was closing too fast. Instead I grabbed the canteen and a sack of food, ran behind the farthest mound, and hid in a place where I was out of sight but could still see what was happening.

The vehicle slowed down. As it pulled up even with me, I realized it was the van we had seen earlier at the roadblock. The driver was the blond man whom the Chinese soldiers had been interrogating, and in the passenger seat was a woman.

As I watched, they slowed the van to a complete stop and began to talk. I thought about going out and talking to them but immediately felt a flash of fear. What if the soldiers had alerted them about us, insisting that they be notified if we were seen? Would they turn me in?

The woman opened her door slightly as though to get out, still talking with the man. Had they spotted the Jeep? My mind was running wild. I decided that if she got out and came over, I would just start running. That way, they would only get the Jeep, and I could put some distance between myself and this place before the officials came.

With that thought in mind, I looked back at the van. The two were gazing toward the mounds, an expression of concern on their faces. They looked at each other one more time before the woman slammed her door shut, and they sped away toward the west. I watched the van crest the small hill to my left and disappear.

Somewhere inside me I felt disappointed. Maybe they could have helped me, I thought. I considered running to the Jeep and overtaking them, but I dismissed the idea. Better not to tempt fate, I concluded. It was more prudent to go back to my original plan and attempt to find my way back to Lhasa and home.

After about a half hour I returned to the Jeep and started the engine. The crow to my left squawked and flew down the road in the direction the Dutch van had gone. I turned the other way and headed back toward Zhongba, taking a series of small roadways, hoping to bypass the main streets and the restaurant. I made it several more miles before I reached the top of a hill. I slowed the Jeep as I crested the peak so that I could survey the long expanse of highway in the distance.

When I got into a position to see, I was shocked. Not only was there a new roadblock set up half a mile down the mountain with dozens of soldiers, but I could count four big trucks and two Jeeps filled with troops heading my way, closing fast.

I quickly turned the Jeep around and raced back in the direction I'd come, hoping they wouldn't see me. I knew I would be lucky to outpace them. I reasoned that I should travel farther west as fast as I could, then bear south and east. Perhaps there were enough small roads that I could get back to Lhasa that way.

I darted across the main street and into a series of side roads, again heading south. I turned a curve and realized I was going the wrong way. I had inadvertently returned to the main road again. Before I could stop, I was less than one hundred feet from another Chinese checkpoint. There were soldiers everywhere. I pulled over to the side of the road and put on the brake, then slid way down in the seat.

Now what? I thought. Prison? What would they do to me? Would they think me a spy?

After a few moments I noticed that the Chinese seemed oblivious to my presence, even though I was parked in plain sight. Old cars and carts and even pedestrians on bikes kept passing me, and the soldiers would stop them all and ask for identification, checking their papers and sometimes searching them. Yet they paid me no attention at all.

I glanced to the right and realized that I was parked just short of a driveway that led up to a small, stone house, several hundred feet away. To the left of the house was a small lawn of uncut grass, and beyond the grass, I could see another street.

Just at that moment a large truck drove past and stopped right in front of me, blocking my view of the checkpoint. Moments later a blue Toyota Land Cruiser driven by another blond man came up and pulled around the truck. Next I heard loud talking and shouts in Chinese. The vehicle seemed to be backing up as if to try to turn around, but the soldiers swarmed it. Although my line of sight was blocked, I could hear angry shouts in Chinese interspersed by fearful pleas in English that carried a Dutch accent.

"No, please," the voice said. "I'm sorry. I'm a tourist. Look, I have a special license to drive on the road."

Another car pulled up. My heart leaped in my chest. It was the same Chinese official I'd seen at the restaurant earlier. I slipped farther down in my seat, trying to hide as he walked right past me.

"Give me your papers!" he asked the Hollander in perfect English.

As I listened, I noticed something move to my right and peered through the passenger window to see what it was. The driveway down toward the house appeared to be bathed in a warm luminous glow, the exact same glow I had witnessed when Yin and I had escaped just outside Lhasa. The dakini.

The Jeep was idling, so all I had to do was pull slowly to the right and down the drive. I was barely breathing as I passed the house and drove through the grass to the next street and turned left. A mile farther I turned left again, heading north out of town on the side street I had taken earlier. Ten minutes later I was back at the mounds, pondering what to do. Down the road to the west, I heard another crow caw. Instantly I decided to head in that direction, the way I could have been traveling all along.

The road led up a steep rise, crested, and then settled into a long straight-away along a rocky plain. I drove for several hours as the afternoon light began to fade. There were no cars or people to be seen anywhere and almost no houses. Half an hour later it was completely dark, and I was thinking about finding a place to pull over for the night when I noticed a narrow gravel drive heading off to my right. I slowed the Jeep and looked more closely. There was something just to the side of the driveway. It looked like an item of clothing.

I stopped the Jeep and shined a flashlight out through the window. It was a parka. My parka. The one I had left in the restaurant just before the Chinese had come.

Smiling, I switched off the light. Yin must have placed my jacket here. I got out of the Jeep, picked it up, and drove up the narrow road with the headlights off.

The drive led about half a mile up a gradual incline to a small house and barn. I drove cautiously. Several goats looked at me from across a fence. On the porch of the house, I noticed a man sitting on a stool. I stopped the Jeep and he stood up. I knew that silhouette. It was Yin.

I got out of the Jeep and ran up to him. He met me in a stiff embrace, smiling.

"I'm glad to see you," he said. "You see, I said you were being helped."

"I was almost caught," I replied. "How did you get away?"

A nervousness returned to his face. "The women at the restaurant are very cunning. They saw the Chinese officers and hid me in the oven. No one ever looked in there."

"What do you think will happen to the women?" I asked.

He met my eyes but said nothing for a long moment.

"I do not know," he replied. "Many people are paying a high price for helping us."

He looked away and pointed to the Jeep. "Help me bring in some food and we'll make something to eat."

As Yin made a fire, he explained that after the police had left, he had gone back to his friends' house and they had suggested this old house as a place for him to stay while they looked around for another vehicle.

"I knew that you might become overwhelmed by fear and try to get back to Lhasa," Yin added. "But I also knew that if you decided to continue on this journey, you would eventually try to head northwest again. This was the only road, so I placed your jacket there hoping it would be you who saw it and not the soldiers."

"That was quite a risk," I said.

He nodded as he put the vegetables in a heavy boiler filled with several inches of water and hung it on the metal hook over the fire to steam. Yak dung flames lapped at the bottom of the pan.

Seeing Yin again seemed to take much of my fear away, and as we sat down in old dusty chairs by the fire, I said, "I have to admit that I did try to get away. I thought it was my only chance to survive."

I went on to tell him everything that had happened—everything, that is, except the experience of the light around the house. When I got to the part where I was in the mounds and the van came by, he sat up in his chair.

"You are sure it was the same van we saw at the roadblock?" he asked pointedly.

"Yes, it was them," I replied.

He looked totally exasperated. "You saw the people we had seen before and you didn't speak with them?" His face had an edge of anger. "Don't you remember me telling you about my dream, about us meeting someone who could help us find the gateway?"

"I didn't want to take a chance that they would report me," I protested.

"What?" He stared at me, then leaned over and held his face in his hands for a moment.

"I was petrified," I said. "I can't believe I've gotten myself in this situation. I wanted out. I wanted to survive."

"Listen to me closely," Yin said. "The chances of your getting out of Tibet now by fleeing are very slim. Your only chance of surviving is to go forward, and to do that, you have to use the synchronicity."

I looked away, knowing he was probably right.

"Tell me what happened when the van approached," Yin said. "Every thought. Every detail."

I told him the van had stopped, and when it did, I immediately grew afraid. I described how the woman acted as if she wanted to get out, but changed her mind and they left.

He shook his head again. "You killed the synchronicity with a misuse of your prayer-field. You set your field with fearful expectations and it stopped everything."

I looked away.

"Think about what was happening," Yin continued, "when you heard the van approaching. You had two choices: You could have thought about that occurrence as a threat or as a potential aid. Certainly you have to consider both. But once you recognized the van, that should have told you something. The fact that it was the same van that we had seen earlier at the crossroads is meaningful, especially since these same people created the diversion that allowed us to go by without being seen. From that point of view, they had already helped you and now were there to possibly help you again."

I nodded. He was right. Clearly I had blown it.

Yin looked away, distracted by his own thoughts, then said, "You completely lost your energy and positive expectation. Remember what I told you at the restaurant? Setting a field for synchronicity is a matter of putting yourself in a particular state of mind. It is easy to think about synchronicity intellectually, but unless you enter the state of mind where your prayer-field will help, all you will do is glimpse the coincidences every once in a while. In some situations that is enough and you will be led forward for a time, but eventually you will lose your direction. The only way to establish a constant flow of synchronicity is to stay in a state where your prayer field keeps this flow moving toward you—a state of conscious alertness."

"I'm still not sure how to get into this state of mind."

"One must stop and remind oneself to assume an attitude of alertness every moment. One must visualize that one's energy is going out and bringing just the right hunches to you, the right events. You have to expect them to occur at any moment. We set our fields to bring us synchronicity by being ever vigilant, always expecting the next encounter. Every time you forget to keep yourself in this state of expectation, you must catch yourself and remember.

"The more you stay in this state of mind, the more the synchronicity will increase. And, eventually, if you keep your energy high, this posture of conscious alertness will become your prevailing attitude toward life. The legends say the prayer extensions will eventually be second nature to us. We will set them in the morning as routinely as getting dressed. That is the place you must reach, the state of mind where you have this expectation constantly."

He paused and looked at me for a moment.

"When you heard the vehicle coming toward you, you immediately went into fear. From the sounds of it, they were intuiting that they should stop at the mounds, although they probably had no idea why. But when you went into fear, thinking that they were possibly the bad guys, your field actually went out and had an effect on them, entering their fields and probably making them feel something was amiss, that they were doing something wrong, so they took off."

What he was telling me was fantastic, but it felt true to me.

"Tell me more about how our fields affect people," I said.

He shook his head. "You're getting ahead of yourself. The effect of our fields on other people is the Third Extension. For now just concentrate on setting a field for synchronicity, and not going into fearful thoughts. You have a tendency to expect the worst. Remember when we were on our way to Lama Rigden's and I left you alone, you saw a group of refugees and they would have led you right to the Lama's monastery if you had only talked to them. But instead you figured they were going to turn you in and you missed the synchronicity. This negative thinking is a pattern with you."

I just looked at him, feeling tired. He smiled and didn't mention any of my mistakes again. We talked casually about Tibet for most of the evening, going outside at one point to look up at the stars. The sky was clear and the temperature barely freezing. Above us were the brightest stars I had ever seen and I commented to Yin about it.

"Of course they look big," he said. "You are standing on the rooftop of the world."

The next morning I slept late and went through a series of tai chi movements with Yin. We waited for as long as we could for

Yin's friends, but they never showed up. We realized we'd have to risk going with only one vehicle, after all, and loaded up the Jeep, pulling out right at noon.

"Something must have happened," Yin said, looking over at me. He was trying to be strong, but I could tell he was worried.

We were heading up the main road again through a thick, sand-blown haze that had covered most of the landscape and obscured our view of the mountains.

"It will be hard for the Chinese to see us in this," Yin remarked.

"That's good," I said.

I had been wondering how the Chinese knew we had been at the restaurant in Zhongba, so I asked Yin what he thought.

"I'm sure it was my fault," he said. "I told you how much anger and fear I felt toward them. I'm sure my prayer-field was bringing me what I was asking for."

I looked hard at him. This was too much.

"Are you telling me," I asked, "that because you were fearful, your energy went out and somehow brought the Chinese to us?"

"No, not merely the fear. We all get a general kind of fear. That's not what I mean. I'm talking about letting my mind go into fearful visions of what might happen, what the Chinese might do. I've seen them operate in Tibet for so long, I know their methods. I know how they oppress individuals through intimidation. I allowed myself to see them coming for us in my mind, as a little vision, and I wasn't doing anything to counteract that image.

"I should have caught myself and envisioned in my mind that they would no longer be so antagonistic toward us, and then held that expectation. My fear in general was not what brought them. I went unconscious and held a specific image, a specific expectation that they would come in on us. That was the problem. If you hold a negative image too long, it can eventually come true."

I was still awed by the whole idea. Could this be correct? For a long time I had observed that people who feared a particular event—a burglary at their house, for instance, or getting a particular disease or losing a lover—often experienced just that occurrence in their lives. Was this the effect Yin was describing?

I remembered the fearful image I'd had earlier in Zhongba, when Yin had left to find someone to go with us. I had imagined being alone in the Jeep, driving around lost, which is exactly what had ended up happening. A chill went through me. I had been making the same mistake as Yin.

"Are you saying that everything that happens to us that's negative is the result of our own thoughts?" I asked.

He frowned. "Of course not. Many things merely happen in the natural course of living with other human beings. Their expectations and actions play a part too. But we do have some creative influence, whether we want to believe it or not. We have to wake up and understand that in terms of our prayer-energy, an expectation is an expectation, whether it is based on fear or faith. In this case, I wasn't monitoring myself closely enough. I told you my hatred of the Chinese was a problem."

He turned and our eyes met.

"Also, remember what I told you," he added, "that at these higher levels of energy, the effect of our prayer-field is very quick. Out there in the ordinary world, individuals still have a mix of fear images and success images, so they tend to cancel each other out and keep the effect low. But at these levels, we can affect what happens very quickly, even though a fear image will eventually collapse the strength of our field.

"The key is to make sure your mind is focused on the positive path of your life, not on some fearful expectation. That's why the Second Extension is so important. If we make sure we stay in a state of conscious alertness for the next synchronicity, our minds stay on the positive and off our fear and doubt. Do you see what I mean?"

I nodded but said nothing.

Yin focused again on the road. "We have to use this power right now. Stay as alert as you can. We could pass the van very easily in this haze and we don't want to miss them. You're sure they were heading in this direction?"

"Yes," I said.

"Then if they stopped to spend the night, the way we did, they couldn't be that far ahead."

All morning we traveled, still heading northwest. As much as I tried to keep it up, I couldn't stay in the state of conscious alertness Yin was describing. Something wasn't right. Yin noticed and kept looking over at me.

Finally he turned and said, "Are you sure you're expecting the full synchronistic process?"

"Yeah," I replied. "I think so."

He frowned slightly and continued to glance over at me.

I knew what he was getting at. Both in Peru and later in the Appalachians with the Tenth Insight, I'd experienced a process to synchronicity. Each of us at any one point has a primary question about our lives, something we are inquiring into, given our particular life situation. In our case, the question was how we might find the Dutch van, and then Wil and the gateway.

Ideally, once we recognize the central question in our lives, we will have a guiding thought or an intuition about how to answer it. We find ourselves with a mental image that would suggest going somewhere, taking some action, saying something to a stranger. Again, ideally, if we follow that intuition, coincidences will occur to give us information pertaining to our question. This synchronicity leads us further down our life path . . . and, in turn, to a new question.

"What do the legends say about this?" I asked.

"They say," Yin replied, "that humans will eventually learn that their prayer power can greatly influence the flow of their lives. By using the force of our expectations, we can bring forth the process of synchronicity more frequently. But we have to stay alert for the whole process, beginning with the next intuition. Are you consciously expecting an intuition?"

"I haven't gotten anything yet," I said.

"But are you expecting one?" he pressed.

"I don't know. I wasn't really thinking about intuitions."

He nodded. "You must remember that this is part of setting your field of prayer for synchronicity. You must stay alert and expect the whole process to come forth: the question, getting an intuition and following it, and looking for the coincidences. Remind yourself to expect it all, be alert for it all, and if you do, your energy will go out ahead of you and help bring the flow."

He shot me a smile meant to uplift my spirits.

I took in a few breaths, feeling my energy begin to return. Yin's mood was contagious. My alertness sharpened.

I smiled back at him. I was for the first time appreciative of who Yin was. At times he was as fearful as me, and often he was too blunt, but his heart was into this journey and he wanted more than anything to succeed. As I thought about this, I slipped into a daydream of Yin and me walking through rocky sand dunes at night, somewhere near a river. There was a glow in the distance, a campfire, that we wanted to reach. Yin was leading and I was glad to follow.

I looked over at him again. He was staring hard at me.

I realized what had happened.

"I think I just got something," I said. "I had the thought of us walking toward a campfire. Do you think that means anything?"

"Only you would know," he said.

"But I don't know. How am I supposed to know?"

"If your thought was a guiding intuition, it would have something to do with us looking for the van. Who was at the campfire? What was the feeling?"

"I don't know who was there. But we wanted to reach the campfire very badly. Is there a sandy area nearby?"

Yin pulled the Jeep off the road and stopped. The haze was beginning to lift.

"This landscape is all rocky sand for another hundred miles," Yin said.

I shrugged my shoulders. "What about a river? Is there a river somewhere close?"

Yin's eyes lit up. "Yes, just past the next town, Paryang, about a hundred and fifty miles up ahead."

He paused for a moment, smiling broadly.

"We must stay very alert," he said. "It is our only lead."

We made good time, reaching Paryang by sunset. We drove straight through town and then on for another fifteen miles, where Yin turned off to the right on a track road. It was almost completely dark, but we could see the river half a mile ahead.

"There is a checkpoint up ahead," he explained. "We have to go around it."

As we approached the river, the road narrowed and became extremely rutted.

"What's that?" Yin asked, stopping the Jeep and backing up.

Off in a rocky clearing to our right, barely visible, was a vehicle. I rolled down the side window so we could see more clearly.

"It's not a van," Yin said. "It's a blue Land Cruiser."

I strained to see.

"Wait a minute," I said. "That's the vehicle I saw at the roadblock when we were separated."

Yin shut off our headlights, and the darkness seemed to engulf us.

"Let's go on a little farther," he said, pulling the Jeep forward through the deep ruts for several hundred more feet.

"Look!" I said, pointing. To our left was the van, parked between large rocks. No one was around.

I was about to get out when Yin lurched the Jeep forward and parked it out of sight several hundred yards to the east.

"Better to hide our vehicle," he commented, locking it up as we got out.

We returned to the van and looked around.

"The footprints go in this direction," Yin said, gesturing toward the south. "Come on."

I walked behind him as we made our way through the large rocks and sand. A three-quarter moon lit our way. After about ten minutes he looked at me and sniffed. I could smell it too: the smoke of a fire.

We walked another fifty yards in the darkness until we saw a campfire. A man and a woman were huddled around it. It was the Dutch couple I had seen in the van. The river was just beyond.

"What do we do?" I whispered.

"We'll have to announce ourselves," he said. "You had better do it so they will be less afraid."

"We don't know who they are," I said, resisting.

"Go ahead, tell them we are here."

I looked at them more closely. They were dressed in fatigues and thick cotton shirts. They looked like mere tourists, trekking in Tibet.

"Hello," I said in a loud voice. "We're glad to see you."

Yin looked at me askance.

The two people jumped up and stared closely as I emerged from the darkness. Smiling broadly, I said, "We need your help."

Yin followed, bowing slightly, and said, "We're sorry to disturb you, but we're looking for our friend Wilson James. We were hoping you could help us."

They were both in shock, not believing we had walked into their camp this way. But slowly the woman seemed to realize we were harmless and offered us a place to sit beside the fire.

"We do not know Wilson James," she said. "But the man we are here to meet tonight does know him. I've heard him mention the name."

Her companion nodded, looking very nervous. "I hope Jacob can find us. He is hours late."

I was about to tell them that we had seen the Land Cruiser parked not too far away when the expression on the man's face changed. He looked petrified. His eyes were glued to something behind me. I jerked around. Back in the direction of the vehicles, the terrain had come alive with other vehicles and headlights and dozens of voices speaking in Chinese, all moving in our direction.

The man leaped to his feet and extinguished the fire. He grabbed several packs and ran out of the camp with the woman.

"Come on," Yin said, trying to catch up to them. Within several minutes they had disappeared in the darkness. Finally Yin gave up. Behind us, the lights were getting closer, and we huddled by the river.

"I think I can make my way around to our Jeep," Yin said. "If we are lucky they haven't found it yet. You head north, upstream, for about a mile, and try to outdistance them. You'll find another road there that comes down to the river's edge. Listen for me and I'll pick you up."

"Why can't I go with you?" I asked.

"Because it is too dangerous. One man might get through, but two would be seen."

Reluctantly I agreed, and began to make my way through the rocks and gravel mounds in the moonlight, using my flashlight only when absolutely necessary. I knew Yin's plan was crazy, but it seemed to be our only chance. I wondered what would have been learned if we had talked longer to the Dutch couple or met the other man. After about ten minutes I stopped to rest. I was cold and tired.

I heard a rustling ahead of me. I strained to hear. Someone was definitely walking. It must be the Dutch couple, I thought. Slowly I made my way forward until I caught up with the sound. Twenty feet away, I could see the silhouette of only one person, a man. I knew I had to say something or risk losing him.

"Are you Dutch?" I stammered, thinking that this might be the man the couple was waiting to meet.

He froze and said nothing, so I repeated the question. It sounded silly, but I thought perhaps I would get some kind of response.

"Who is it?" came a reply.

"I'm an American," I said. "I've seen your friends."

He turned and looked at me as I struggled through the rocks to reach him. He was young, perhaps twenty-five, and looked terrified.

"Where did you see my friends?" he asked, his voice shaking.

As he focused on me, I could feel how afraid he was. A wave of fear swept through my body, too, and I struggled to keep up my energy.

"Back downstream," I replied. "They told us they were waiting for you."

"Were the Chinese there?" he asked.

"Yes, but I think your friends got away."

He looked even more panicked.

"They told us," I said quickly, "that you know a man I'm looking for, Wilson James."

He was backing up. "I've got to get out of here," he said, turning to leave.

"I've seen you before," I said. "You were detained at a checkpoint in Zhongba."

"Yes," he said. "You were there?"

"I was behind you in the traffic. You were being questioned by a Chinese official."

"That's right," he replied, nervously looking in all directions.

"What about Wil?" I asked, struggling to stay calm. "Wilson James. Do you know him? Did he tell you anything about a gateway?"

The young man didn't say anything. His eyes were glazed over with fear. He just turned and ran back through the rocks, heading farther upstream. I chased him for a while but he soon disappeared into the darkness. Finally I stopped and looked back toward where the van and our Jeep were parked. I could still see lights and hear muffled voices.

I turned and headed north again, realizing full well that I had blown my chance. I had gotten no information from him. I tried to shrug off the failure. More important was finding Yin and trying to get away myself. Eventually I found the old road, and minutes later I heard the faint sound of a Jeep.

5

THE CONTAGION OF AWARENESS

I stretched out as best I could in the cramped vehicle. I was completely exhausted and I wondered how Yin had the strength to drive. I knew we had been fortunate. As Yin had supposed, the Chinese military had seemed disorganized and nonchalant about their search. They had posted a single guard at the Dutch couple's van while the others halfheartedly searched in the other direction, totally overlooking our Jeep. Yin had managed to start it up without making much noise and move around them unde-tected to pick me up at the river.

At this point Yin was still driving with the headlights off and staring intently though the windshield to see the darkened road.

After a moment he glanced over at me. "The young Dutchman you saw didn't tell you anything?"

"That's right," I said. "He was too frightened. He just ran away."

Yin was shaking his head. "This is my fault. If only I had told you about the next prayer extension, the Third. You would have been more effective at getting the information."

I began to question what he meant, but he waved me off with his hand.

"Just remember where you are," he instructed. "You have experienced the First Extension: connecting with the energy and letting it flow through you, visualizing that it forms a field of energy that flows ahead of you wherever you go. The Second Extension, as I have been explaining, is setting your field of energy so that it will enhance your life flow. You do this by staying ever alert and expectant.

"The Third Extension is setting your prayer-field to go out and increase the energy and vibrational levels of others. When your prayer-field reaches other people in this way, they feel a hit of spiritual energy, clarity, intuition, and they will be more likely to give you the right information."

Again I knew exactly what he was getting at. Under the tutorship of Wil and Sanchez in Peru, I had explored how to send energy to other people as a new ethical stance toward others. Now Yin seemed to be clarifying how to do this more effectively.

"I know what you mean," I said. "I was taught that there's a higher-self expression that can be found on every person's face. If we speak to that self, that expression, our energy helps to lift a person into higher-self awareness."

"Yes," Yin responded, "but this effect is increased if one knows how to extend one's prayer-field the way the legends explain. We must expect our prayer-field to go out in front of us and increase other people's vibration at a distance, even before we are close enough to see their faces."

I regarded him questioningly.

"Look at it this way: If you are truly practicing the First Extension, the energy is coming into you and you are seeing the world more as it really is—colorful, vibrant, beautiful, like a magic forest or a colorful desert. Now, to practice the Third Extension, you must consciously visualize that your energy is overflowing into the field of everyone around you and lifting their vibration so that they, too, begin to see the world as it really is. Once this happens, they can slow down and sense the synchronicity. After setting our fields in this manner, it is easier to observe the higher-self expression on the faces of others."

He paused and looked over at me as though he had just thought of something else.

"Remember, too," he continued, "that there are pitfalls that must be avoided when you uplift someone. Each face is a pattern of features, like an . . . uh . . . inkblot, and you can see many things there. You can see the anger of your abusive father, the aloofness of an uncaring mother, or the face of someone who has threatened you. This is a projection from your past, a perception created by a traumatic situation that has colored how you expect others to act. When you see someone who even slightly resembles someone who has done you wrong, the tendency is to expect that person to be the same way.

"This problem is very important to understand and must be monitored closely. We all must get beyond expectations dictated by our past experiences. Do you understand?"

I nodded, anxious for him to proceed.

"Now, think again of what happened to you at the hotel in Kathmandu. We must look at that more closely. Didn't you say that the man at the pool changed the mood of everyone when he sat down?"

I nodded again, thinking back. That was exactly right. The man had seemed to bring a new mood into the pool area before he had even said a word.

"That occurred because his energy was already set to enter the energy fields of others and give them a positive boost. Think about how that felt, exactly."

I looked away for a moment, trying to re-create what had happened. Finally I said, "Everyone in the area seemed to go from a state of irritation and discontent to a state of mind that was more open and conversant. It's hard to explain."

"His energy opened you up to explore something new," Yin continued, "instead of being stuck in dread or despair or whatever else you people were feeling."

Yin stopped talking briefly, looking closely at me.

"Of course," he went on, "it could have gone the other way. If the man hadn't been strong enough in his energy as he walked into the pool area, he might have been overwhelmed by the low energy state of the rest of you and been brought down to your level. That's what happened to you when you met the young Hollander. He was terrified and his fear affected you. You let his mood prevail.

"You see, the energy fields of all of us mix together out there, and the strongest ones prevail. That's the unconscious dynamic that characterizes the human world. The state of our energy, our prevailing expectations, no matter what they are, go out and influence everyone else's mood and attitude. The level of awareness between humans, and all the expectations that go with it, are contagious.

"This fact explains the great mysteries of crowd behavior, why decent people, influenced by a few who are in great fear or anger, can get caught up in lynchings, riots, or other despicable deeds. It also explains why hypnosis works and why movies and television have such great influence on the weak-minded. The prayer-field of each person on Earth intermingles with all the others, creating all the norms and group affiliations and national mind-sets and ethnic hostilities that we see out there."

Yin smiled. "Culture is contagious. Just travel to a foreign land and see how the people not only think differently but feel differently, as a matter of mood and outlook.

"This is a reality that we must understand and master. We must remember to consciously use the Third Extension. When we are relating to people and find we are taking on their mood, being overcome with their expectations, we have to go back and fill up again and overflow very consciously until the mood elevates. If only you could have done this with the young Dutchman, you might have found out about Wil."

I was impressed. Yin seemed to have a full mastery of this information.

"Yin," I said, "you're a scholar."

His smile faded.

"There's a difference between knowing how all this works," he replied, "and being able to do it."

I must have slept for hours because when I awoke, the sun was out and the Jeep was pulled off onto a flat area above the road. I stretched, then collapsed back into the seat. For a few minutes I stared out past several mounds of rocks at the gravel highway below us. A nomad leading a horse and small wagon trod by, but otherwise the road was empty. The sky was crystal-clear, and from somewhere behind us I could hear a bird's call. I took a breath. Some of the tenseness from the day before had eased.

Yin slowly began to move and then sat up, glancing over at me with a smile. He stepped out of the Jeep and stretched, then pulled a camp stove from the back and put on a pan of water for oatmeal and tea. I joined him and again tried to follow him through a set of difficult tai chi exercises.

From behind us, we heard a vehicle racing down the road. We waited behind a rock as the Land Cruiser sped by, both of us recognizing it at the same time.

"That's the young Hollander," Yin said, running to the Jeep. I grabbed the camp stove and threw it into the back and hopped into the vehicle as Yin was turning around.

"We'll be fortunate to catch him at that speed," Yin commented as we gave chase.

We drove over a small hill and down into a narrow valley, finally catching a glimpse of the vehicle cruising down the road several hundred yards ahead of us.

"We have to reach out to him with our prayer-energy," Yin said.

I took a deep breath, visualizing my energy outflowing up the road and into the Land Cruiser and having an effect on the young man. I imaged him slowing down and stopping.

As I sent the image, the vehicle actually sped up, pulling away from us. I was confused.

"What are you doing?" Yin yelled, looking over at me.

"I'm using my field to make him stop."

"Don't use your energy that way," Yin said quickly. "It has the opposite effect."

I looked at him blankly.

"What do you do," Yin asked, "when someone tries to manipulate you into doing something?"

"I resist it," I said.

"That's right," Yin went on. "At the unconscious level the Hollander can feel you trying to tell him what to do. He feels manipulated, and that gives him the sense that whoever is behind him is up to no good, which produces more fear and adds to his determination to flee.

"All we can do is visualize our energy reaching out and increasing his level of vibration overall. This allows him to more fully overcome the fear and get in touch with his higher-self intuitions, which hopefully will lead him to be less afraid of us and to maybe risk a conversation. That's all we can do with our prayer-energy. To do anything else is to presume that we know his best life course, but only he knows that. Perhaps it will be that his higher intuition—once we send him enough energy—is to dump us and get out of the country. We have to be open to that. All that we can do is help him make the decision from the highest possible level of energy."

We rounded a curve in the road, and the blue Land Cruiser was nowhere to be seen. Yin slowed down. To our right was a smaller road that seemed to stand out in appearance.

"That way!" I said, pointing.

A hundred yards ahead, at the bottom of a small hill, was a wide but shallow tributary. In the middle was the Dutchman's vehicle, racing its engine, spinning its wheels, and spattering mud, but going nowhere. It was stuck.

The young man glanced back at us and opened the door, preparing to run. But when he recognized me, he shut the engine off and got out in the knee-deep water.

As we pulled our Jeep alongside, Yin looked at me closely, and I could tell from his expression that he was reminding me to use my energy. I nodded to him.

"We can help you," I said to the young man.

He eyed us suspiciously for a moment, but gradually warmed as Yin and I got out and pushed the fender of the Land Cruiser as he gunned the engine. Its wheels spun for a moment, spewing mud against my pants leg, then it leaped out of the hole and crossed to the other side of the river. We followed in our Jeep. The young man looked at us for a moment, as though deciding whether to drive away, but got out and walked back toward us. As he approached, we introduced ourselves. He told us his name was Jacob.

As we spoke, I began to look for the wisest expression I could find on his face.

Jacob was shaking his head, still terrified, and spent several minutes finding out who we were and querying us further about his missing friends.

"I don't know why I came to Tibet," he said finally. "I always thought it was too dangerous. But my friends wanted me to come with them. I have no idea why I agreed. My God, there were Chinese soldiers everywhere. How did they know we were going to be there?"

"Did you ask for directions from anyone you didn't know?" Yin asked.

He looked hard at us. "I did. Do you think they told the soldiers?"

Yin nodded, and Jacob seemed to go deeper into panic, looking around in all directions nervously.

"Jacob," I asked, "I have to know, did you meet Wilson James?"

Jacob still seemed unable to focus. "How do we know the Chinese aren't right behind us?"

I tried to catch his eye, finally managing to get him to look at me. "This is important, Jacob. Do you remember seeing Wil? He looks Peruvian, but he speaks with an American accent."

Jacob still looked confused. "Why is this important? We must find a way out of here."

As we listened, Jacob made several suggestions about where we might camp until the Chinese left the area, or better yet, how we might make a mad dash across the Himalayas into India.

I continued to visualize my energy going into him and to focus on his face, looking for an expression of calmness and wisdom in his features, especially in his eyes. Finally he began to look at me.

"Why do you want to find this man?" he asked.

"We believe that he needs our help. He is the man who asked me to come to Tibet."

He looked at me for a moment, apparently trying to focus.

"Yes," he said finally. "I did meet your friend. He was in the lobby of a hotel in Lhasa. We were sitting across from each other and started talking about the Chinese occupation. I've been incensed about the Chinese for a long time, and I guess the reason I came here was that I wanted to do something, anything. Wil told me he had seen me three times that day at various locations in the hotel, and that it meant something. I didn't know what he was talking about."

"Did he mention a place called Shambhala?" I asked.

He looked interested. "Not exactly. He mentioned something in passing, something about Tibet not being freed until Shambhala was understood. Something like that."

"Did he mention a gateway?"

"I don't think so. I can't remember much of the conversation. It was really very brief."

"What about his destination?" Yin asked. "Did he mention where he was going?"

Jacob looked away, thinking, then said, "I think he mentioned a place called—Dormar, I think it was—and something else about the ruins of an old monastery there."

I looked at Yin

"I know that place," he said. "It's in the far northwest, four or five days travel. It will be rough . . . and cold."

The thought of having to travel that far into the wilderness of Tibet sent my energy crashing.

"Do you want to come with us?" Yin asked Jacob.

"Oh no," he said. "I have to get out of here."

"Are you sure?" Yin pressed. "The Chinese seem to be very active right now."

"I can't," Jacob said, looking away. "I'm the only one left to contact my government and look for my friends, if I can find a way to get help."

Yin scribbled out something on a piece of paper and handed it to Jacob.

"Find a phone and call this number," Yin said. "Mention my name and give them a return number. Once they check you out, they will call and tell you what to do." Yin went on to tell Jacob the best way back to Saga, and we walked with him as he made his way back to his Land Cruiser.

Once he had climbed inside, he said, "Good luck . . . I hope you find your friend."

I nodded.

"If you do," he added, "then maybe it will turn out that this is why I came to Tibet, huh? So that I could help."

He turned and started the Cruiser, looked at us one more time, and drove away. Yin and I hurried back to our vehicle, and as we pulled back onto the main road, I noticed he was smiling.

"Do you think you understand the Third Extension now?" he asked. "Think about all that it entails."

I looked at him for a moment, pondering his question. The key to this extension, it seemed, was the idea that our fields can boost others, lifting people into a higher awareness where they can tap into their own guiding intuitions. What expanded this idea for me, beyond anything I had heard in Peru, was the concept that our prayer-field flows out in front of us, and that we can set it to uplift everyone around us—even though we aren't talking to them directly or even seeing their faces. We can do this by visualizing fully that it is happening—by expecting it.

Of course, one has to be totally noncontrolling with this energy; otherwise it backfires, as I had seen when I tried to make Jacob stop his vehicle. I mentioned all this to Yin.

"What you are understanding is the contagious aspect of the human mind," Yin explained. "In a sense, we all share minds.

Certainly we have control over ourselves and can pull back, cut ourselves off, think independently. But as I said earlier, the prevailing human worldview is always a giant field of belief and expectation. The key to human progress is to have enough people who can beam a higher expectation of love into this human field. This effort allows us to build an ever higher level of energy, and to inspire each other toward our greatest potential."

Yin seemed to relax for a moment and smiled over at me.

"The culture of Shambhala," he said, "is built around setting such a field."

I couldn't help smiling back. This journey was beginning to make sense in a way I couldn't yet articulate.

The next two days went smoothly, with no sign of the Chinese military. Still on the southern route heading northwest, we crossed another river near the top of Mayun-La, a high mountain pass. The scenery was spectacular with icy mountain peaks on each side of the road. We spent the first night at Hor Qu in an unmarked roadhouse that Yin knew about and proceeded the next morning toward Lake Manasarovar.

As we approached the lake, Yin said, "Here we will have to be very careful again. The lake, and Mount Kailash farther on, are key destinations for people from all over the region: India, Nepal, China, as well as Tibet. It is a holy place like no other. There will be many pilgrims as well as Chinese checkpoints."

Several miles ahead Yin pulled off on an old track and we made our way around one of the checkpoints, then caught sight of the lake. I looked at Yin, who smiled. The sight was unbelievably beautiful: a huge turquoise pearl set against the rocky, brown-olive terrain, all framed against the snow-covered mountains in the background. One of the mountains, Yin pointed out, was Kailash.

As we drove past the lake, we could see numerous groups of pilgrims standing around large poles strung with flags.

"What are those?" I asked.

"Prayer flags," Yin replied. "Placing flags symbolizing our prayers has been a tradition in Tibet for centuries. The prayer flags are left to flap in the wind, and this sends the prayers they contain continually out to God. Prayer flags are also given to people."

"What kind of prayers do the flags contain?"

"Prayers for love to prevail in all of humanity."

I was silent.

"Ironic, isn't it?" Yin added. "The culture of Tibet is totally dedicated to the spiritual life. We are arguably the most religious anywhere. And we have been attacked by the most atheistic government on Earth—that of China. It is a perfect contrast for all the world to see. One vision or the other will prevail."

Without talking further, we drove through another small town and then into Darchen, the closest town to Mount Kailash, where Yin hired two mechanics he knew to check our Jeep for any potential problems. We made camp with the other locals as close to the mountain as we could get without arousing suspicion. I couldn't keep my eyes off the icy peaks.

"From here, Kailash looks like a pyramid," I said.

Yin nodded. "What does that tell you? It has power."

As the sun sank below the horizon, we observed an amazing sight. A magnificent sunset filled the western sky with layer upon layer of peach-colored clouds, and at the same time, the sun below the horizon still shone on the face of Mount Kailash, turning its snowy slopes into a dazzling spectacle of yellow and orange.

"All through history," Yin said, "great emperors have traveled thousands of miles on horseback or by carrier to witness these sights in Tibet. It was thought that the first light in the morning and the last in the evening had great rejuvenating and visionary powers."

I nodded as he talked, unable to look away from the majestic light around me. I did feel rejuvenated, and almost calm. In front of us, toward Kailash, the flat valleys and low foothills were bathed in alternate layers of shadow and light brown reflections, providing an eerie contrast to the sunlit higher ridges, which seemed to glow from within. The sight was surrealistic, and for the first time I realized why the Tibetans were so spiritual. The light of this land alone led them inexorably into a fuller awareness.

Early the next morning, we were on our way again, and in five hours we had reached the outskirts of Ali. The sky was overcast and the temperature was falling rapidly. Yin made several turns on nearly impassable roads in order to miss the main part of town.

"This is mainly a Chinese area now," Yin said, "with bars and strip joints for the soldiers. We want to get through without anyone noticing us."

When we hit a decent road again, we were already north of town. At one point I caught sight of a newly built office building with several newer trucks parked outside. No one was moving anywhere on the grounds.

Yin saw it at the same time and turned off the main road into an old driveway and stopped.

"That's a new Chinese facility," he said. "I didn't know it was here. Watch and see if anyone there observes us as we go by."

At that moment a wind came up and it began to snow heavily, helping to obscure our identity. As we drove on, I looked very closely at the grounds. Most of the windows of the building were draped.

"What is that place?" I asked.

"An oil exploration station, I think. But who knows?"

"What's with this weather?"

"It looks like a storm is coming in. This could help us."

"You're thinking they might be looking for us up here, aren't you?" I asked.

He looked at me with a profound sadness, which turned into a furious anger.

"This is the town where my father was killed," he said.

I shook my head. "It's terrible that you had to see that."

"It has happened to thousands of Tibetans," he added, staring straight ahead.

I could feel his hatred.

He shook his head. "It is important not to think about that. We have to avoid such images. Especially you. As I told you before, I may not be able to control my anger. You must do better than me with this problem, so that you can go on alone if necessary."

"What?"

"Listen to me closely," he said. "You must understand exactly where you are. You have learned the first three extensions. You have been able to consistently raise your energy and create a strong field, but like me, you still fall into fear and anger. There are some other things I can tell you about anchoring your out-flow of energy."

"What do you mean by anchor?" I asked.

"You must stabilize your flow of energy better, so that it is coming out of you into the world strongly no matter what your situation is. When you do this, all three of the extensions that you have learned become a constant mind-set and way of life."

"Is this the Fourth Extension?" I asked.

"It is the beginning of the Fourth. What I am about to tell you is the last information we have about the extensions. The rest of the Fourth Extension is known clearly only to those in Shambhala.

"Ideally the extensions should work together like this: Your prayer-energy should come from your divine connection within and flow out in front of you, bringing forth the expected synchronicity and uplifting everyone it touches into his or her higher self. In this way it maximizes the mysterious evolution of our lives, and the awareness of and completion of our individual missions on this planet.

"Unfortunately we hit bumps in the road, challenges that bring on a state of fear, which, as we have discussed, brings on doubt and thus collapses our fields. Worse, this fear can bring on negative images, bad expectations, which can help create what we fear in our lives. What you must learn now is a way of anchoring your higher energy so that you stay in the positive flow more often.

"The problem with fear," Yin went on, "is that it can be very subtle and sneak up on us quickly. You see, a fear image is always about some outcome we don't want. We fear failing, embarrassing ourselves or our families, losing our freedom or someone we love, or our own lives. The difficult part is that when we begin to feel such fear, it often turns into anger, and we use this anger to martial our forces and fight back against whoever we feel is the threat.

"Whether we are feeling fear or anger, we have to realize that these emotions come from one source: those aspects of our lives we want to hold on to.

"The legends say that since fear and anger come from being concerned that we are going to lose something, the way to avoid these emotions is to be detached from all outcomes."

We were well north of town now and the snow was falling even heavier. Yin was straining to see the road and glanced only briefly at me as he talked.

"Take our case, for instance," he said. "We are looking for Wil and the gateway to Shambhala. The legends would say that at the same time we set our fields to expect just the right intuitions and events to guide us, we should detach totally from any particular outcome. This is what I was getting at when I cautioned you about being too attached to whether Jacob stopped or not. The importance of detachment is the great message of the Buddha and the gift to humanity provided by all the Eastern religions."

I was familiar with the concept, but at the moment I was having trouble seeing its value.

"Yin," I protested, "how can we detach completely? This idea often sounds like an ivory tower theory to me. It may be a matter of life and death that we help Wil. How can we not care about that?"

Yin pulled the Jeep off the road and stopped. Visibility was now near zero.

"I didn't say not to care," he continued. "I said not to be attached to any particular outcome. What we get in life is always slightly different from what we want anyway. To be detached is to realize that there is always a higher purpose that can be found in any event, in any outcome. We can always find a silver lining, a positive meaning, that we can build on."

I nodded. This was a concept I knew from Peru.

"I understand," I said, "the value of looking at things that way generally, but doesn't such an outlook have its limits? What if we are about to be killed or tortured? It's hard to be detached about that or to see a silver lining."

Yin stared at me hard. "But what if being tortured is always the result of us not being detached enough during the events leading up to such a critical situation? Our legends say that when we learn detachment, our energy can remain high enough to avoid all these extremely negative occurrences. If we can stay strong, always expecting the positive, whether the outcome was exactly what we thought or not, then miracles begin to happen."

I couldn't believe this. "Are you saying that everything bad that happens to us occurs because we missed some synchronistic opportunity to avoid it?"

He looked at me with a smile. "Yes, that's exactly what I'm saying."

"But that's awful. Doesn't that assign blame, say, to someone who has a terminal disease, thinking that it's his own fault he's sick because he missed the opportunity to find healing?"

"No, there is no blame. We all do the best we can. But what I have told you is a truth we must accept if we are to reach the highest levels of prayer-energy. We must keep our fields as strong as possible, and to do this we must always believe, with a powerful faith, that we will be saved from such problems.

"At times we will miss something," he continued. "Human knowledge is incomplete, and we may die or be tortured because of a lack of information. But the truth is this: If we had all the knowledge that humans will eventually have, we would always be guided out of a perilous situation. We reach our greatest power when we assume this is the case already. This is the way we can stay detached and flexible and build a powerful field of expectation."

It was all beginning to make sense. Yin was telling me we had to assume that the synchronistic process would always take us out of harm's way, that we would know ahead of time which moves to make, because that ability is our destiny. If we believe that, sooner or later it will become a reality for all humans.

"All the great mystics," Yin went on, "say that operating from total faith is important. The apostle John in your Western Bible describes the result of this kind of faith. They put him in a vat of boiling oil and he was unharmed. Others were placed with hungry lions, and they remained safe. Are these merely myths?"

"But how high does our faith have to be to achieve this level of invulnerability?" I asked.

"We have to reach a level approaching those in Shambhala," Yin replied. "Don't you see how it all fits together? If our ongoing prayer expectation is strong enough, we both expect synchronicity and send energy to others so that they can also expect synchronicity. The level of energy keeps going up. And in the meantime there is always the dakini . . ."

He looked away quickly, apparently horrified that he had mentioned these beings again.

"What about the dakini?" I asked.

He was silent.

"Yin," I pressed, "you have to tell me what you mean. How do the dakini fit into all this?"

Finally he took a breath and said. "I'm telling you only what I myself understand. The legends say the dakini are understood only by those in Shambhala, and that we must be very careful. I can't tell you more."

I looked at him angrily. "Well, we'll just have to find out later, won't we, when we reach Shambhala?"

He looked at me with great sadness. "I already told you I have had too much experience with the Chinese military. My hate and anger erode my energy. If at any time I see that I am holding you back, I will have to leave, and you will have to go on alone."

I stared at him, not wanting to contemplate that idea.

"Just remember," he continued, "what I said about being detached and about trusting that you will always be guided past any danger."

He paused a moment as he started the Jeep and drove on through the blowing snow.

"You can bet," he finally said, "that your faith will be tested."

6

THE PASSAGE

After traveling north for forty minutes, Yin turned onto a well-worn truck road and headed toward a high mountain chain twenty or thirty miles away. The snow continued to get heavier. Faintly at first and then steadily growing louder, a low drone rose above the engine noise and wind.

Yin and I looked at each other as the sounds finally became recognizable.

"Helicopters," Yin yelled, pulling the Jeep off the track and through an opening in the rocks. The Jeep bounced wildly. "I knew it. They have some way of flying in this weather."

"What do you mean you knew it?"

As the sounds rose above us, I thought I heard two craft. One was hovering directly over us.

"This is my fault," Yin screamed over the noise. "You must get out! Now!"

"What?" I yelled. "Are you crazy? Where will I go?"

He yelled into my ear. "Don't forget to stay alert. Do you hear me? Keep going northwest to Dormar! You must get to the Kun-lun Mountains!"

119

With one deft move he opened my door and shoved me out.

I landed on my feet, then tumbled several times into a snow-bank. I sat up and struggled to catch sight of the Jeep, but it was already driving away and the blowing snow obscured my view. A wave a sheer panic filled me.

At that moment a movement to the right caught my attention. Through the snow I could see the figure of a tall man about ten feet away, dressed in black yak leather pants and a sheepskin vest and hat. He was standing still, staring intensely at me, but his face was partially covered by a wool scarf. I recognized those eyes. From where? After a few more seconds he looked up toward the helicopter, which was making another pass, and dashed away.

Without warning, three or four terrific explosions erupted in the direction the Jeep had gone, blowing rocks and snow all over me and filling the air with a choking smoke. I got up and stag-gered away as several more small explosions echoed around me. The blowing air was now completely filled with some kind of noxious gas. My head began to spin.

I heard the music before I was completely conscious. It was a classic Chinese composer I had heard before. I jerked awake and realized I was in an elaborate, Chinese-style bedroom. I sat up in the ornate bed and pushed back the silk sheets. I was clothed only in a hospital gown and I had been bathed. The room was at least twenty by twenty feet, and each paneled wall had a different mural. A Chinese woman was peeking at me through the crack in the door.

The door opened, and in walked an erect Chinese military officer in full uniform. A chill went through me. It was the same official I had now seen several times. My heart pounded. I tried to extend my energy, but the sight of the officer completely deflated me.

"Good morning," the man said. "How do you feel?"

"Considering I was gassed," I replied, "pretty good."

He smiled. "It has no lasting effect, I assure you."

"Where am I?"

"You are in Ali. The doctors have seen you and you are fine. But I must ask you some questions. Why were you traveling with Yin Doloe and where were you going?"

"We wanted to visit some of the old monasteries."

"Why?"

I decided not to tell him any more. "Because I'm a tourist. I have a visa. Why was I attacked? Does the American Embassy know I'm being held?"

He smiled, and looked ominously into my eyes. "I am Colonel Chang. No one knows you are here, and if you have broken our laws, no one can help you. Mr. Doloe is a criminal, a member of an illegal religious organization which is perpetrating a fraud in Tibet."

My worst fears seemed to be happening.

"I don't know anything about that," I said. "I would like to call someone."

"Why are Yin Doloe and the others looking for this Shambhala?"

"I don't know what you're talking about."

He took a step closer to me. "Who is Wilson James?"

"He's a friend of mine," I said.

"Is he in Tibet?"

"I think so, but I haven't seen him."

Chang looked at me with a hint of disgust and, without saying anything else, turned and walked out.

This is bad, I thought, very bad. I was about to get out of bed when the nurse returned with half a dozen soldiers, one of them pushing what looked like a huge iron lung, only it was bigger and standing on tall, wide legs, apparently so that it could be rolled up over someone who was lying in a bed.

Before I could say anything, the soldiers were holding me and rolling the machine over my body. The nurse turned it on, producing a mild humming noise and a bright light directly over my face. Even with my eyes closed I could see the light move from right to left across my head, like the scanner of a copy machine.

As soon as the machine stopped, the soldiers rolled the device away and left the room. The nurse lingered a moment looking me over.

"What was that?" I stammered.

"Just an encephalograph," she said in careful English as she reached into a cabinet and pulled out my clothes. They had been cleaned and folded neatly.

"What was it for?" I pressed.

"To check everything, to make sure you are all right."

At that moment the door opened again, and Colonel Chang returned. He picked up a chair by the wall and set it near my bed.

"Perhaps I should tell you what we are faced with here," he said as he sat down in the chair. He looked tired. "There are many religious sects in Tibet, and many of their adherents seek to give the impression around the world that they are a religious people being oppressed by the Chinese. And I admit that our early policies in the 1950s, and during the Cultural Revolution, were harsh. But these policies have been changed in recent years. We are trying to be as tolerant as we can, given that the official policy of the Chinese government is atheism.

"These sects must remember that Tibet has changed as well.

Many Chinese live here now and have always lived here, and many of them are not Buddhists. We must all live together. There is no way that Tibet can ever return to Lamaist rule.

"Do you understand what I am saying? The world has changed. Even if we wanted to give Tibet its freedom, it would not be fair to the Chinese."

He waited for me to say something, and I thought about confronting him with the government policy of importing Chinese nationals into Tibet in order to dilute the Tibetan culture. Instead I said, "I think they just want to be free to pursue their religion without interference."

"We have allowed some of that, but they are always changing what they are doing. Once we think we know who is in charge, the situation changes. I think we are arriving at a good relationship with parts of the official Buddhist hierarchy, but then there are the Tibetan expatriates in India, and this other group that Mr. Doloe is a part of, the one that follows some cryptic verbal knowledge and is stirring up all this talk about Shambhala. It is distracting to the people. There is much important work to be done in Tibet. The people are very poor. The quality of life must be raised."

He looked at me and grinned. "Why is this legend of Shambhala being taken so seriously? It seems almost juvenile, the idea of children."

"The Tibetans believe that there is another, more spiritual reality beyond the physical worlds we can see, and that Shambhala, while here on this Earth, lies in this spiritual realm." I couldn't believe I was risking a debate with him.

"But how could they think this place exists?" he continued. "We have surveyed every inch of Tibet from the air and from satellites, and we have seen nothing."

I was silent.

"Do you know where this place is supposed to be?" he pressed. "Is that why you are here?"

"I would love to know where it is," I said, "or even what it is, but I'm afraid I don't. I also don't want to be in trouble with the Chinese authorities."

He was listening intently, so I continued. "In fact, all this scares the hell out of me and I would really rather leave."

"Oh no, all we want is for you to share what you know," he said. "If such a place exists, if it is a hidden culture, we want to know this information. Share your knowledge with us and let us help you. Perhaps there is a compromise that could be made."

I looked at him for a moment and said, "I would like to contact the American Embassy, if that's okay."

He tried to hide his impatience, but I could see it clearly in his eyes. He stared at me for a moment longer, then walked to the door and turned around.

"That's not necessary," he said. "You are free to go."

Minutes later I was walking down the streets of Ali, zipping up my parka tightly. It was not snowing now but it was very cold. Earlier I had been forced to dress in front of the nurse and then escorted from the house. As I continued to walk, I went through the contents of my pockets. Surprisingly everything was there: a knife, my wallet, a small bag of almonds.

I felt light-headed and fatigued. Was this from the anxiety? I wondered. The effects of the gas? The altitude? I tried to shake it off.

Ali was a modern town, with numerous Chinese and Tibetans walking the streets, and vehicles everywhere. Its well-kept buildings and stores were slightly disconcerting, given the terrible roads and conditions we had just traveled through to get here. Looking around, I could see no one who I thought might be able to speak English, and after several blocks I began to feel even more light-headed. I had to sit down beside the road on an old cement block. The growing fear almost became a panic. What was I to do now? What had happened to Yin? Why had the Chinese colonel let me go like that? It made no sense.

With that thought, a full image of Yin appeared in my mind, and I felt a reminder. I was letting my energy collapse. The fear was overwhelming me and I had forgotten to do anything about it. I took a deep breath and attempted to raise my energy.

A few minutes later I began to feel better, and my eyes fell on a large building several blocks away. It had a sign on the side in Chinese that I couldn't read, but as I focused on the shape of the building, I got the distinct impression that it was a guesthouse or small hotel. I felt elated. There would be a phone there perhaps, maybe even other tourists I could hook up with.

I stood up and walked in that direction, careful to keep an eye on the streets around me. In a few minutes I was several doors away from the Shing Shui guesthouse, but I felt hesitant and looked around carefully. No one seemed to be following me. When I was almost to the door, I heard a noise. Something had landed in the snow. I looked around. I was standing on the street directly across from a narrow alleyway, alone except for several old men walking in the other direction twenty feet away. I heard the noise again. It was close. As I was looking down at my feet, I saw a small stone fly out of the alley and plop into the snow.

Taking one step forward, I tried to look down the shadowed opening. I took several more steps, trying to adjust my eyes.

"It's me," a voice said.

I knew immediately it was Yin.

I rushed into the alley, finding him leaning against a brick wall.

"How did you know where I was?" I asked.

"I didn't know," came his reply. "I was just guessing." He slid down the wall and sat down, and I noticed his parka was burned on the back. When he moved his arm, I saw a patch of blood on his shoulder.

"You're hurt!" I said. "What's wrong?"

"It's not that bad. They dropped a concussion bomb and I hit rocks when I was thrown from the Jeep. I managed to crawl away before they landed. I saw them take you and load you onto a truck headed back here. I figured if you got away, you would head toward the largest guesthouse. What happened to you?"

I told Yin about waking up in the Chinese house and being interrogated by Colonel Chang, then released.

"Why did you push me out of the Jeep?" I asked.

"I told you before," Yin replied. "I can't control my fearful expectations. My hatred for the Chinese is too great. They are able to follow me." He paused. "Why did they release you?"

"I don't know," I replied.

Yin moved slightly and grimaced in pain. "Probably because Chang senses that he can follow you too."

I was shaking my head. Could this be real?

"He wouldn't know how it works, of course," Yin continued, "but when you expect the soldiers to come, your expectation actually gives his ego the thought to approach where you are. He probably thinks it is some power in him."

He looked at me hard. "You must learn from my problem. You must master your thoughts."

Yin looked at me a moment longer, then, holding his arm, led me down the alley, through a narrow gap between two buildings, and into what looked to be an abandoned building.

"We need to get you to a doctor," I said.

"No!" Yin said forcefully. "Listen to me. I will be fine. There are people here who can help me. But I can't go with you to the ruins of the old monastery; you will have to go there by yourself."

I turned away, fear swelling inside me. "I don't think I can do that."

Yin looked alarmed. "You must control your fear, return to detachment. You are needed to help find Shambhala. You must go on."

He struggled to sit up, grimacing as he moved closer to me. "Don't you understand that the Tibetan people have suffered much? Yet they have waited for the day that Shambhala would be known to all the world." He squinted as his look found my eyes. "Think of how many people have helped us get this far. Many of them have risked everything. Some may be imprisoned, even shot."

I lifted up my hand and showed it to him; it was shaking. "Look at me. I can barely move."

Yin's eyes were piercing. "Don't you think your father was terrified when he struggled out of that landing craft and ran onto the beaches of France in World War II? Just like all the others? But he did that! What if he hadn't? What if all the rest of them hadn't? That war could have been lost. Freedom for everyone could have been lost.

"We in Tibet have lost our freedom, but what is happening now is about more than just Tibet. It is about more than you or me. It is about what must happen for all the sacrifices of many generations to be honored. Understanding Shambhala, learning to use the prayer-fields at this moment in history, is next in the evolution of humankind. It is the great chore of our whole generation. If we fail, then we let down everyone who came before us."

Yin grimaced in pain, then looked away. Tears were forming in his eyes.

"I would go if I could," he added. "But now I think you are our only chance."

We heard the sound of big trucks and saw two large troop carriers drive by.

"I don't know where to go," I said.

"The old monastery is not that far," Yin replied. "They can be reached in a long day's travel. I can get someone to take you."

"What am I supposed to do there? You said earlier that I would be tested. What did you mean by that?"

"In order to get through the gateway, you will have to fully allow divine energy to flow through you and set your field in the way you have learned. Know this field goes out from you and has an effect on what happens. Most importantly, control your fear images, and stay detached. You still fear certain outcomes. You don't want to lose your life."

"Of course I don't want to lose my life," I said, almost yelling. "I have a lot to live for."

"Yes, I know," he replied gently. "But those are very dangerous thoughts. You have to abandon all thoughts of failing. I can't do that, but I think you can. You have to be sure with all your faith that you're going to be saved, that you are going to succeed."

He paused to see if I understood.

"Anything else?" I asked.

"Yes," he said. "If all else fails, continue to affirm that Shambhala is helping you. Look for the . . ."

He stopped, but I knew what he meant.

The next morning I was in the cab of an old, four-wheel-drive truck, squeezed in between a herdsman and his four-year-old son. Yin had known exactly what to do. In spite of his pain, we had sneaked across several blocks to an old adobe brick house, where we were given a hot meal and a place to spend the night.

He stayed up late talking to several men. I could only suppose that the men were members of Yin's secret group, but I asked no questions. We had risen early, and minutes later the farm truck had driven up and I had climbed aboard.

We were now traveling along a snow-covered dirt road, circling ever higher into the mountains. As the truck bounced along, we turned a corner and reached an overlook where we could see the place where Yin and I had said good-bye. I asked the driver to slow the truck so I could see.

To my horror, the whole area below was filled with military vehicles and soldiers.

"Wait a minute," I said to the driver. "Yin may need help. We have to stop."

The old man shook his head. "Must go! Must go!"

He and his son talked excitedly in Tibetan, occasionally looking at me, as though they knew something I didn't. He sped up the truck and we traveled through a pass and started down through the mountains.

A pang of fear erupted in my stomach. I was torn about what to do. What if Yin had escaped and needed me? On the other hand, I thought I knew what Yin would have wanted. He would have insisted that I go on. I tried to keep my energy up, but part of me wondered if all the talk about gateways and Shambhala might turn out to be just a myth. And even if it was true, why would I be allowed to enter and not someone else, like Jampa or Lama Rigden? Nothing made sense.

I shrugged off those thoughts and tried to keep my energy high, gazing out at the snow-covered peaks. I watched closely as we traveled through several small towns, including Dormar. Finally after eating a lunch of cold soup and dried tomatoes, I fell asleep for a long time. When I awoke, it was late afternoon and large snowflakes were falling again, soon covering the road with a fresh coating of whiteness. As we continued to travel, the terrain grew ever more mountainous and I could tell the air was growing thinner. Approaching in the distance was yet another tall range of mountains.

That must be the Kunlun range, I thought, the one Yin had mentioned. Part of me continued to disbelieve that all this was happening. But another knew it was, and that I was alone now, facing the monolithic Chinese presence, with all its soldiers and atheistic skepticism.

From behind us, I heard the low drone of a helicopter. My heart began to pound, but I kept my alertness.

The herdsman seemed oblivious to the threat and drove on for another thirty minutes, then smiled and pointed up ahead. Through the falling snow I could see the darker outlines of a large stone structure sitting atop one of the first ridges. Several walls on the left side were collapsed. Behind the monastery rose huge spires of snow-covered rock. The monastery was three or four stories tall, even though its roof had long since rotted away, and I looked closely for a moment for any sign of people or movement. I saw nothing. It seemed to have been completely abandoned for a long time.

At the base of the mountain, five hundred feet below the monastery, the truck stopped and the man pointed up toward the ruined structure. I hesitated, looking out at the blowing snow. He gestured again, urging me on with his excited expression.

I grabbed the pack Yin had prepared for me from the back of the truck. I started up the hill. The temperature was growing slightly colder, but I hoped that with the tent and sleeping bag, I would not freeze to death. But what about the soldiers? I watched the truck move out of sight and listened carefully, hearing nothing but the wind.

I looked around and found a rock stairway up the hill and

started to climb. After about two hundred feet I stopped and looked back toward the south. From here I could see nothing but white mountains for miles.

As I approached the monastery, I could now see that it actually wasn't on a hill of its own but stood on a large precipice extending out from the mountain behind it. The path led right to the opening that was once a large door, and I carefully walked in. Large, hued stones lay scattered around the dirt floor, and I was facing a long hallway that ran the length of the structure.

I walked down the hall past several rooms that opened up on both sides of me. Finally I came to a larger room that had a doorway to the back side of the monastery. In fact, half its rear wall had collapsed, and more stones, some of them as big as tables, lay on the ground outside.

Out of the corner of my eye, I saw a movement near the collapsed wall. I froze. What was that? Cautiously, I walked to the opening and looked outside in all directions. It was about a hundred feet from the door to the sheer rock face of the mountain. No one seemed to be around.

As I continued to look, I saw another vague movement, also out of the corner of my eye. This time it was farther away, near the base of the mountain face. A chill ran through me. What was going on? What was I seeing? I thought about grabbing my pack and running back down the hill, but I decided against it. I was definitely frightened, but my energy was remaining strong.

I focused as best I could through the falling snow and headed for the cliffs where I thought I had seen the movement. When I arrived, I could find nothing. The cliff walls were laced with vertical crevices, including one very large one that at first looked like a narrow cave. On closer inspection, I saw it was only several feet deep, too shallow for anyone to hide, and filled with snow. I looked around for footprints, and although the snow was ten or twelve inches thick, I could find none but my own.

The snow was falling much harder now, so I walked back to the monastery and found a corner of the room that still had an overhang of stone in place that protected me from the snow and wind. A pang of hunger hit me, and I crunched some carrots as I broke out the small gas stove and heated some freeze-dried vegetable soup Yin had placed in my pack.

As it was simmering, I thought about what was happening. There was only an hour left until dark, and I had no idea why I was up here. I looked through my pack and found no flashlight of any kind. Why hadn't Yin packed one? The gas in the stove wouldn't last through the night; I had to find some firewood or yak dung.

My mind was already playing tricks on me, I thought. What might happen if I had to spend the entire night up here in total darkness? What if these old walls began to fall in the wind?

As soon as I had that thought, I heard a crumbling sound at the far end of the monastery. I walked out to the hall, and just as I looked, I saw a huge stone crash to the ground.

"Jesus," I said aloud. "I have to get out of here."

I turned off the stove and grabbed the other gear and ran out the back into the blowing snow. I quickly realized I would have to find shelter, so I ran back to the mountain cliffs, hoping I had missed a crevice or overhang large enough to camp in.

When I reached the cliffs, I searched in vain for an opening. None of the crevices were deep enough. The wind howled. At one point a huge clump of snow fell from one of the rocks and landed at my feet. I looked up at the tons of accumulating snow that was lining the sides of the mountain above me. What if there was an avalanche here? In my mind's eye I could see the snow rolling down the mountain.

Again, as soon as I had that thought, I heard a rumbling sound above me and to the right. I grabbed the gear and ran back toward the monastery just as a thunderous roar filled the air and snow rolled down the mountainside fifty feet away. I ran as fast as I could and collapsed into the snow halfway back to the monastery, terrified. Why was all this happening?

With that thought, a memory of Yin came to my mind. He was saying. "At these levels of energy, the effect of your expectations is immediate. You will be tested."

I sat up. Of course! This was the test. I wasn't controlling my fear images. I ran back to the old monastery and ducked inside. The temperature was falling rapidly, and I knew I had to risk staying inside. Setting my gear down, I spent several minutes imaging the stones staying in place.

A shiver of cold ran through me. Now, I thought, I have to do something about this cold. I pictured myself sitting beside a warm fire. Fuel. I had to find some fuel.

I walked out to look over the rest of the monastery. I had only reached the hallway when I was stopped cold in my tracks. I could smell smoke, the smoke of burning wood. Now what?

Slowly I walked down the hallway, looking in each room as I came to it, finding nothing. When there was only one room left, I peered around the doorway. In the corner was a burning campfire and a store of wood.

I stepped in and looked around. No one was here. This room had another doorway leading outside, and more of a roof overhead. It felt much warmer. But who built this fire? I walked to the outside opening and looked around at the snow. Still no tracks. I was turning around, heading for the door, when in the half-light I saw a tall figure standing at the edge of the doorway. I tried to focus on him directly, but I could see him only at the peripheral edges of my sight. I realized it was the same man I had seen in the snow when Yin had pushed me from the Jeep. I tried to focus on him directly again and he vanished. The hair on the back of my neck stood up and a chill went through me. I couldn't believe what was happening.

Cautiously I walked through the doorway and peered down the hall in both directions, seeing nothing. I thought again about fleeing the monastery and going down the mountain, but I knew the temperature was still falling fast and if I did I would likely freeze to death. My only option was to go get my stuff and stay by this fire. So I retrieved my gear and returned, peering nervously around every corner.

As I sat down, a gust of wind whipped the fire and blew ash everywhere, and I watched the flames for a moment as they caught back up. I had imaged a fire and then it had manifested. But it was too much to believe that my field could be that strong. There was only one explanation. I was being helped. The figure I saw was a dakini.

As eerie as it all was, that realization eased my mind, and I threw more wood on the fire and finished my soup, then unpacked my sleeping bag. After a few minutes I lay down and fell into a deep sleep.

When I awoke, I looked around wildly. The fire had died down and the first light of dawn was emerging outside. The snow was falling just as hard as the night before. Something had awakened me. What?

I heard the dull drone of helicopters growing louder, heading toward me. Jumping to my feet, I gathered my things. In seconds the helicopters were directly overhead, adding to the swirling wind.

Without warning, half the monastery began to crumble and fall inward, creating a storm of blinding dust. I felt my way out the back opening and ran outside, abandoning my gear. The blizzard was still blowing horizontal snow, and I could only see a few yards in front of me, but I knew if I continued to run in this direction, I would soon come to the mountain face I had seen the day before.

I struggled on until I could see the rocky slope. It was directly in front of me about fifty feet away, but in the dawn light I knew it shouldn't be this visible. It was as if the mountain was bathed in a soft, slightly amber color, especially near one of the large crevices I had seen before.

I stared a moment longer, knowing what it meant, then took off running toward the light as more of the monastery fell in behind me. When I reached the cliff wall, the helicopters seemed to be directly overhead. What was left of the old monastery completely crashed down behind me, shaking the ground and dislodging the snow in the crevice nearest to me, revealing a narrow opening. It was a cave, after all!

I stumbled through the passageway and into total darkness, feeling my way ahead. I found the back wall and then another opening that was less than five feet high. It bent to the right and I crawled through it, glimpsing the smallest ray of light ahead, far in the distance. I struggled forward.

At one point I tripped over a large rock and feel headfirst onto the dirt and gravel floor, skinning my elbow and arm, but the fading sound of the helicopters drove me onward. I shook off the pain and continued moving in the direction of the light. After I had traveled several hundred feet, I could still see the tiny opening, but it seemed no closer. I continued on for most of an hour, feeling my way toward the tiny illumination ahead of me.

Finally the light seemed to be getting closer, and as I got to within ten feet of it, I was abruptly met with a blast of warmer air and the fragrance that I had smelled before at the monastery.

In the distance somewhere I also heard a loud, melodious human cry that reverberated though my body, bringing forth an inner warmth and euphoria. Was this the call Lama Rigden had mentioned? The call of Shambhala.

I climbed up over the last remaining rock and stuck my head through the opening. Before me was an unbelievable sight. I was facing a large, pastoral valley and clear blue sky. Beyond the valley were huge, snowcapped mountain peaks. All were strikingly beautiful in the bright sunlight. The temperature was chilly but temperate, and green plants were growing everywhere. In front of me the hill sloped gently down toward the valley floor.

As I walked through the opening and started down the hill, I felt overwhelmed by the energy of the place and began to have trouble focusing. Lights and colors were swirling together and I felt myself slump to my knees. Out of control, I began to roll down the hill. I rolled and rolled, almost as though I was half-asleep, losing all sense of time.

7

ENTERING SHAMBHALA

I felt someone touching me, human hands wrapping me up and carrying me somewhere. I began to feel safe, even euphoric. After a while, I smelled the sweet fragrance again, only now it was all-consuming, filling my consciousness.

"Try to open your eyes," a female voice said.

As I struggled to focus, I was able to make out a figure of a large woman, perhaps six and a half feet tall. She was pushing a cup toward my face.

"Here," she said. "Drink this."

I opened my mouth and took in a warm, tasty soup made from tomatoes, onions, and some kind of broccoli that was sweet. As I drank, I realized my taste perception was enhanced. I could discern every flavor precisely. I drank most of the cup, and within moments my head cleared and I could again focus on everything around me.

I was in a house, or what seemed to be a house. The temperature was warm and I was lying on a lounger made from a blue-green fabric. The floor was a smooth brown stone tile, and numerous plants in ceramic pots were sitting close by. Yet above me were blue sky and the overhanging branches of several large trees. The dwelling didn't seem to have a roof or outside walls.

"You should be feeling better now. But you must breathe." The woman spoke in fluent English.

I looked at her, spellbound. She was Asian in appearance, dressed in a colorful, embroidered Tibetan ceremonial dress and soft-looking, simple slippers. Judging from the depth of her gaze and the wisdom in her voice, she was about forty years of age, but her body and movements gave her the appearance of a much younger person. And while her body was perfectly proportioned and beautifully shaped, every feature was exceptionally large.

"You must breathe," she repeated. "I know that you know how to do this or you wouldn't be here."

Finally I understood what she meant, and began to breathe in the beauty of my surroundings and envisioned the energy coming into me.

"Where am I?" I asked. "Is this Shambhala?"

She smiled approvingly and I couldn't believe the beauty of her face. It was slightly luminous.

"Part of it," she replied. "What we call the rings of Shambhala. Farther to the north are the holy temples."

She went on to tell me her name was Ani, and I introduced myself as she looked down on me.

"Tell me how you got here," she said.

In a rambling way I told her the whole story, beginning with a brief description of my talk with Natalie and Wil, the Insights, and my trip to Tibet, including meeting Yin and Lama Rigden and hearing about the legends, and then finally finding the gateway. I even mentioned my perceptions of the light, apparently the work of the dakini.

"Do you know why you are here?" she asked.

I looked at her for a moment. "All I know is that I was asked to come by Wil and that it was important to find Shambhala. I was told there is knowledge here that is needed."

She nodded and looked away, thinking.

"How did you learn such good English?" I asked, feeling weak again.

She smiled. "We speak many languages here."

"Have you seen a man named Wilson James?"

"No," she said. "But the gateway can enter the rings at other places. Perhaps he is here somewhere." She had walked over to the potted plants and was pulling one of them closer to me. "I think you must rest awhile. Try to absorb some energy from these plants. Set in your field the intention that their energy is coming in and then go to sleep."

I closed my eyes, following her instructions, and within moments I drifted off.

Sometime later a swooshing noise aroused me. The woman was standing in front of me again. She sat down on the edge of the lounger.

"What was that noise?" I asked.

"It came in from outside."

"Through the glass?"

"It's not really glass. It's an energy field that looks just like glass, but you can't break it. It hasn't been invented in the outer cultures yet."

"How is it created? Is it electronic?"

"Partially, but we have to participate mentally to activate it."

I looked out at the landscape beyond the house. There were other dwellings spread out over the gently rolling hills and meadows, all the way down to the flat valley. Some had clear outer walls, like Ani's house. Others seemed to be made of wood in a uniquely designed Tibetan style. All were nestled unobtrusively into the landscape.

"What about those houses out there with different architecture?" I asked.

"They're all created by a force field," she said. "We don't use wood or metals any longer. We just create what we want with the fields."

I was fascinated. "What about the internal construction, water and electricity?"

"We do have water, but it manifests right out of the water vapor in the air, and the fields power everything else we need."

I looked outside again, disbelieving. "Tell me about this place. How many people are here?"

"Thousands. Shambhala is a very big place."

Interested, I swung my legs off the lounger and put my feet on the floor, but experienced severe light-headedness. My vision blurred.

She got up and reached behind the lounger and handed me more soup.

"Drink this and breathe in the plants again," she said.

I complied and eventually my energy returned. As I took in more air, everything became even brighter and more beautiful than before, including Ani. Her face had become more luminous now, glowing from within, exactly the way I had seen Wil look at times in the past.

"My God," I said, looking around.

"It's a lot easier to raise your energy here than in the outer cultures," she commented, "because everyone is giving energy to everyone else, and setting a field for a higher cultural level." She said the phrase "higher cultural level" with emphasis, as though it had some greater meaning.

I couldn't take my eyes off the surroundings. Every form, from the potted plants close to me, to the colors of the floor tile, to the lush green trees outside, seemed to glow from within.

"All this seems unbelievable," I stammered. "I feel as if I'm in a science fiction movie."

She looked at me seriously. "Much science fiction is prophetic. What you see is simply progress. We're human just like you, and we're evolving in the same way that you in the outer cultures will eventually evolve, if you don't sabotage yourselves."

At that moment a young boy of about fourteen ran into the room, nodding politely to me, and said, "Pema called again."

She turned to him. "Yes, I heard. Will you get our jackets and one for our guest?"

I couldn't take my eyes off the boy. His demeanor seemed much older than he looked, and his appearance was familiar. He reminded me of someone, but I couldn't remember who.

"Can you come with us?" Ani said, breaking my stare. "This may be important for you to see."

"Where are we going?" I asked.

"To a neighbor's house. Just to check things. She thinks she conceived a child a few days ago, and she wants me to check her out."

"Are you a doctor?"

"We don't really have doctors, because we no longer have the illnesses you are familiar with. We have learned how to keep our energy above that level. I help people monitor themselves and extend their energy and keep it that way."

"Why do you say it's important for me to see?"

"Because you happen to be here at this moment." She looked at me as though I was dense. "Certainly you must understand the synchronistic process."

The young boy returned and I was introduced. His name was Tashi. He handed me a bright blue jacket. It looked exactly like an ordinary parka except for the stitching. In fact, there was no stitching at all. It was as if the pieces of fabric were simply pressed together. And surprisingly, even though the jacket felt just like cotton, it weighed almost nothing.

"How are these made?" I asked.

"They're force fields," Ani said as she and Tashi walked through the wall with a whoosh. I tried to follow and bounced back from what felt like a solid piece of Plexiglas. The boy outside laughed.

With another swoosh, Ani came back in, also smiling.

"I should have told you what to do," she said. "I'm sorry. You must visualize the force field opening for you. Just intend it."

I gave her a skeptical glance.

"Just see it opening in your mind and then walk through."

I did as she described and then walked forward. I could actually see the field open up. It looked like a distortion in the space, something like the heat rays one can see on a highway in the sun. With a swoosh I walked through onto the outside walkway. Ani followed.

I shook my head. Where was I?

Following Tashi, we traveled along a winding path that moved gradually down the slope of the hill. As I glanced back, I saw that Ani's house was almost totally hidden by trees, and then something else grabbed my attention. Near the house was a square, black, metallic-looking unit the size of a large suitcase.

"What is that?" I asked Ani.

"That's our power unit," she replied. "It helps us heat and cool the house and set the force fields."

I was totally confused. "What do you mean, helps you?"

She was walking in front of me as we continued down the slope. She slowed down and let me walk up beside her.

"The power unit by the house doesn't create anything by itself. All it does is amplify the prayer-field you know about to a higher level, so that we can then manifest what we need directly."

I looked at her askance.

"Why does this sound so fantastic?" Ani asked, smiling. "I told you: it is merely progress."

"I don't know," I said. "During all this time of trying to reach Shambhala, I guess I never gave much thought to what it would be like here. I guess I thought it was going to be just a group of high lamas in meditation somewhere. This is a culture with technology. It's fantastic . . ."

"It's not the technology that matters. It's how we have used the technology to help build our mental powers that is important."

"What do you mean?"

"All this is not as outlandish as you think. We merely discovered the lessons of history. If you look closely at the human story, you can see that technology has always been just a precursor for what could eventually be done with the human mind alone.

"Think about it. Throughout history people created technology to enhance their ability to act and to be comfortable in the world. In the beginning it was only pots to hold our food and tools to dig with, then more sophisticated houses and buildings. To create these items, we dug up ores and minerals and fashioned them into what we envisioned in our minds. We wanted to travel more effectively, so we invented the wheel and then vehicles of various sorts. We wanted to fly, so we made airplanes that helped us do it.

"We wanted to communicate more rapidly, over great distances, anytime we wished, and so we invented wires and telegraphs, telephones, wireless radios, and television—to let us see what was happening in another location."

She looked at me questioningly. "See the pattern? Humans invented technology because we wanted to reach out to various places and connect with more people, and we knew in our hearts that it was possible for us to do that. Technology has always been just a stepping-stone to what we can do ourselves, what we knew was our birthright. The true role of technology has been to help us build the faith that we can do all these things ourselves, with our inner power.

"So in the early history of Shambhala, we began to evolve technology to consciously serve the development of the human mind. We realized the true potential of our prayer fields and began to recraft our technology to merely amplify our fields. Here in the rings, we still use the amplification devices, but we are right on the brink of being able to turn them off and just use our prayer-fields to manifest everything we need or want to do. Those in the temples can already do this."

I wanted to ask her more questions, but as we rounded a bend, I saw a wide creek running down the hill to our right. The sound of rushing water echoed ahead.

"What's that sound?" I asked.

"There's a waterfall up there," she said. "Do you feel you need to see it?"

I didn't quite know what she meant.

"Do you mean intuitively?" I asked.

"Of course I mean intuitively," she replied, smiling. "We live by intuition."

Tashi had stopped and was looking back.

Ani turned to him. "Why don't you go tell Pema we're coming."

He smiled and ran on ahead.

We climbed up the rocky slope to our right, moving closer to the stream, and pushed through some thicker, smaller trees until we came to the edge of the water. The stream was twenty-five feet wide and flowing briskly. Through the limbs to our left I could see the water going over a ledge. Ani motioned for me to follow. We walked along the stream and down several tiers of rock until we were just below the falls. From here we could see the fifty-foot drop into a large pool below.

A movement caught my eye, and I moved out to the edge of the rock to look down. To my surprise, through the mist and spray at the end of the pool I could see two people walking toward each other, both surrounded by a soft, pinkish white light. Even though the light wasn't very bright, it was remarkably dense, especially around their shoulders and hips. I strained to make out the full outlines of the two people, and when I did I realized that they were naked.

"So this is what you brought me up here to see?" Ani asked, amused.

I couldn't take my eyes off what was happening. I knew that I was watching the energy fields of a man and a woman. As they approached each other, their fields merged until they were embracing. Finally, ever so slowly I saw another light forming in the midsection of the woman. After a few minutes they separated and the woman felt her stomach. The tiny light grew brighter, and the two embraced again and seemed to be talking, but I could hear nothing but the waterfall. Without warning both people simply disappeared.

I realized that they had been making love and I became embarrassed.

"Who were those people?" I asked.

"I didn't recognize them," Ani replied. "But they're from the region somewhere."

"It looked as though they conceived a child," I said. "Do you think they intended to?"

She burst into a chuckle. "This isn't the outer cultures. Of course they intended to conceive. At these levels of energy and intuition, bringing a soul onto the Earth is a very deliberate process."

"How did they disappear like that?"

"They traveled there by projecting themselves mentally through a travel field. The amplification device allows us to do that. We found that the same electromagnetic field that sends television pictures can be used to actually link the space of a remote location to the space where we are. When we do that, we can simply look at a scene wherever we want, or actually walk through to the other site, using our amplified prayer-field. The wormhole theorists in the outer cultures are already working on such theories now, only they aren't fully conscious of what it will lead to."

I just looked at her, trying to absorb the new information.

"You look overwhelmed," she said.

I nodded, managing a smile.

"Come on, I'll show you at Pema's."

When we arrived, the house was just like Ani's, except that it was built into the side of a hill and had different furniture. I noticed an identical black box outside, and we entered through the force field just as before. We were met by Tashi and another woman, who introduced herself as Pema.

Pema was taller than Ani and slimmer. Her hair was jet black and long. She wore only a long white dress and was smiling, but I realized that something was not quite right. She asked to see Ani alone and they walked into another room, leaving Tashi and me sitting in a living area.

I was about to ask him what was wrong when I felt an electricity in the air behind me. I saw the rippled distortion open just like the one I'd seen in the force field around Ani's house, only this time it appeared in the middle of the room. I blinked, trying to grasp what was happening. As I focused, I saw a field with small plants through the distortion, as though it were a window. To my surprise a man walked through the opening into the room.

Tashi stood up and introduced us. The man's name was Dorjee. He nodded politely to me and asked where Pema was. Tashi pointed toward the bedroom.

"What just happened?" I asked Tashi.

He looked at me with a smile. "Pema's husband arrived from his farm. Can't some of you do this in the outer cultures?"

I told him briefly about the rumors and myths about yogis who could project themselves to distant locations. "But I've never personally seen anything like this," I added, trying to regain my composure. "How is it done exactly?"

"We visualize the place where we want to go, and the amplifier helps us to create a window into that place right in front of us. It also creates an opening back in the other direction as well. That's how we could see where he was before he came through."

"And the amplifier is the black box outside?"

"That's right."

"And all of you can do this?"

"Yes, and it is our destiny to do it without the amplifier."

He stopped and stared at me, then asked, "Will you tell me about the culture you came from, in the outer world?"

Before I could answer, we heard a voice from the bedroom declare, "It's happened again."

Tashi and I looked at each other.

After a few minutes Ani led Pema and her husband out of the bedroom, and they all sat down in the living room beside us.

"I was so certain that I was pregnant," Pema said. "I could see the energy and feel it momentarily, and then within a few minutes, it disappeared. It must be the transition."

Tashi was looking at her intensely, totally fascinated.

"What do you think happened?" I asked.

"We have intuited," Ani said, "that it is some kind of parallel pregnancy and that the child has gone somewhere else."

Dorjee and Pema looked at each other for a long moment. "We'll try again," Dorjee said. "It almost never happens twice in one family."

"We must be going," Ani said, standing up and embracing the couple. Tashi and I followed her out through the force field.

I was still overwhelmed. In some ways the culture here seemed ordinary; in other ways, totally fantastic. I tried to take it all in as Ani led us a dozen or so yards to a beautiful rock ledge overlooking the massive, green valley below.

"How could there be a temperate environment this large in Tibet?" I blurted out.

Ani smiled. "The temperature is controlled with our fields, and to those with less energy we are invisible. Although the legends say that will begin to change when the transition grows near."

I was startled.

"You know about the legends?" I asked.

Ani nodded. "Of course. Shambhala is the original holder of the legends, as well as many prophecies all through history. We help bring spiritual information into the outer cultures. We also knew that it was only a matter of time before you began to find us."

"Me personally?" I asked.

"No, anyone from the outer cultures. We knew that as you generally raised your level of energy and awareness, you would begin to take Shambhala seriously and that some of you would be able to come here. That is what the legends say. At the time of Shambhala's shift, or transition, people from the outer cultures will arrive. And not just the occasional adepts from the East, who have always found us periodically, but people from the West as well, who will be helped to come here."

"You said the legends predict a transition. What is that?"

"The legends say that as the outer cultures begin to understand all of the steps to extending the human prayer-field—how to connect with divine energy and let it flow through with love, how to set your field to bring on the synchronistic process and uplift others, and how to anchor this strong field with detachment—then the rest of what we do here in Shambhala will become known."

"You're talking about the rest of the Fourth Extension?"

She looked at me knowingly. "Yes. That is, after all, what you're here to see."

"Can you tell me what it is?"

She shook her head. "You must take it one step at a time. You must first realize where humanity is going. Not intellectually, but with your eyes and feelings. Shambhala is the model for that future."

I nodded as I looked at her.

"It's time for the world to know what human beings are capable of, where evolution is taking us. Once you grasp it fully, you will be able to extend your field even more, grow even stronger."

She shook her head and added, "But understand that I don't have all the information about the Fourth Extension. I will be able to guide you through some of the next steps, but there is more that is known only by those at the temples."

"What are the temples?" I asked.

"They are the heart of Shambhala. The mystical place you imagined. It's where the real work of Shambhala is done."

"Where are they located?"

She pointed north across the valley at a strange, circular group of mountains in the distance.

150 | The Secret of Shambhala

"Over there past those peaks," she said.

During the time we were talking, Tashi was silent, listening to every word. Ani looked at him and brushed back his hair with her hand. "It was my intuition that Tashi would have been called to the temples by now . . . but he seems to be more interested in life in your world."

I jerked awake, sweating. I had been dreaming of walking through the temples with Tashi and someone else, on the verge of understanding the Fourth Extension. We were in a maze of stone structures, most of them sandy bronze, but out in the distance was a temple that appeared bluish in color. A person in dramatic Tibetan attire was standing outside. In the dream I began running from the Chinese official I had seen several times before. He was chasing me through the temples and they were being destroyed. I was hating him for what he was doing.

I sat up and tried to focus, barely remembering the walk back to Ani's house. I was now in one of her bedrooms and it was morning. Tashi was sitting in front of the bed on a big chair, staring at me.

I took a deep breath and tried to calm down.

"What's wrong?" he asked.

"Just a scary dream," I said.

"Will you tell me about the outer cultures?"

"Can't you just go there through a window or wormhole, or whatever you call it?"

He shook his head. "No, this is not possible, even at the temples. My grandmother intuited that it could be done, but no one has succeeded because of the differences in the energy levels between the two places. Those at the temples can see what is happening in the outer cultures, but that's all."

"Your mother seems to know a lot about the outer world."

"We get our information from those who reside in the temples. They come back often, especially when they sense that someone is ready to join them."

"Join them?"

"Almost everyone here aspires to acquire a place in the temples. It is the greatest honor and an opportunity to influence the outer cultures."

As he spoke, his voice and level of maturity reminded me of someone thirty years old. Even though he was large, it was disconcerting to look at his fourteen-year-old face.

"How about you?" I asked. "So you want to go to the temples?"

He smiled and looked toward the other room as though he didn't want his mother to overhear.

"No, I keep thinking about somehow going to the outer cultures. Will you tell me about them?"

For half an hour I told him as much as I could about the current state of affairs in the world: the way most people lived, the diets most ate, the struggle to institute democracy around the globe, the corrupting influence of money on government, the environmental problems. Far from being alarmed or disappointed, he soaked it all in with enthusiasm.

Presently Ani came into the room, sensed that there was a conversation of note going on, and paused. Neither of us said anything, and I slumped back down on the pillow.

She looked me over.

"We've got to get more energy into you," she remarked. "Come with me."

I put on my clothes and met her in the living area, then followed her outside and around to the back of the house. Here the trees were very large and spaced about thirty feet apart. Between them was a coarse grass, like sage, and dozens of other plants that looked like huge asparagus ferns. She urged me to move my body and I attempted the exercises Yin had showed me.

"Now sit here," she said when I finished. "And raise your energy again."

As she sat beside me, I began to breathe in and focus on the beauty around me, visualizing the energy coming into me from within. As before, the colors and shapes began to stand out very easily.

I looked over at Ani and saw an expression of deeper wisdom on her face.

"That's better," she said. "You still weren't all here yesterday when we visited Pema. Do you remember what happened?"

"Sure," I replied. "Most of it."

"Do you remember what happened when she thought she had conceived?"

"Yes."

"One moment it seemed to have been there and then it was gone."

"What do you think happened?" I asked.

"No one really knows. These disappearances have been occurring for a long time. In fact they began with me, fourteen years ago. At that time, I was sure I was pregnant with twins, a boy and a girl, and then in an instant one of them was gone. I gave birth to Tashi, but I've always felt that his sister was alive somewhere.

"Since then, couples here have routinely had the same experience. They feel sure that they conceived and then suddenly they realize their wombs are empty. All of them go on to have other births, but they never forget what happened. This phenomenon has been occurring with regularity throughout Shambhala all these fourteen years."

She paused for a moment, then said, "It has something to do with the transition, maybe even with you being here."

I looked away. "I don't know."

"Aren't you having any intuitions?"

I thought for a minute and then remembered the dream. I was about to tell her about it, but I couldn't decide what it meant, so I didn't.

"Not really any intuitions," I said. "Just a lot of questions."

She nodded, waiting.

"How does the economy work here? What do most people do with their time?"

"We have evolved to a place where we no longer use money," Ani explained, "and we no longer manufacture or build items like in the outer cultures. Tens of thousands of years ago we came from cultures that made the things they needed, like you do. But as I told you, we gradually came to understand that the true destiny of technology was to be used to develop our mental and spiritual abilities."

I felt the soft sleeve of my parka. "You mean everything you have is a created energy field?"

"That's right."

"What keeps it together?"

"Once created, these fields last for as long as the energy is not disrupted by negativity of some kind."

"What about food?"

"Food can be created in the same way, but we found that food is best grown by individuals in a natural process. Food plants respond to our energy and give it back to us. Of course, we no longer have to eat very much to stay vibrant. Most in the temples don't eat at all."

"What about power? How are the amplifiers powered?"

"Energy is free. A long time ago, we discovered a device using processes that you would call cold fusion. It created virtually free energy for our culture, which liberated us from spoiling the environment and enabled us to automate our mass production of goods. Gradually all our time became focused on our spiritual paths, on synchronistic perception, and on discovering new truths about our existence and providing this information to others."

As she spoke, I recognized that she was describing a human future I first leaned about in the Ninth and Tenth Insights.

"As we developed spiritually here in Shambhala," she went on, "we began to understand that human purpose on this planet was to evolve a culture that is spiritual in all its aspects. And then we realized that we had a greater power within us to help us accomplish what needed to be done. We learned the prayer extensions and used them to further evolve our technology, as I've already explained, to help facilitate this creative power. At this point we live simply in nature and the only technology that remains are these units that help us mentally create everything else we need."

"Did all that evolution take place right here?" I asked.

"No, not at all," she said. "Shambhala has moved many times."

Her statement shocked me for some reason and I questioned her further.

"Oh yes," she clarified. "Our legends are very old and come from many sources. All the myths of Atlantis and the Hindu legends of Meru stem from old civilizations that really existed in the past where the early evolution of Shambhala worked itself out. Developing our technology was the most difficult step, because to place technology fully in the service of our individual spiritual development, everyone must move to a point where spiritual understanding is more important than money and control.

"That takes some time, because people who are locked up in fear—and think they personally need to manipulate the course of human evolution with their egos—often desire to use advances in technology in negative ways, to control others. In many early civilizations, a few controllers tried to subvert the use of the amplification machines by trying to use them to monitor and control other people's thoughts. Many times these attempts ended in war and mass destruction, and humanity had to start all over again.

"The outer cultures face this problem right now. There are people who want to control everyone else by using surveillance, embedded chips, and brain wave scans."

"What about the artifacts of these ancient cultures you're speaking about? Why has almost nothing ever been found?"

"Continental drift and ice have buried much of it, and then, once a culture progresses to a point where material goods are being created mentally, if anything goes wrong, and a wave of negativity brings the energy down, it simply all disappears."

I took a breath and shrugged. Everything she said made perfect sense, yet at the same time was utterly disconcerting. It was one thing to hypothesize human civilization evolving toward a spiritual future. It was quite another to find oneself immersed in a culture that had already reached it.

Ani moved closer. "Just remember that what we have done is the natural course of human evolution. We are ahead of you, but because we have done what we've done, the way can be easier for you in the outer cultures."

She paused and I broke into a grin.

"Your energy looks much better now," she said.

"I don't think I've ever felt this alert."

She nodded. "As I said before, it's the level of energy the individuals here in Shambhala maintain. It's contagious. There are so many people here who know how to bring energy into themselves and project it outward to others that it creates a multiplying effect, where everyone takes in the prayer-energy they have received from others and sends it out to everyone else again. Do you see how it grows? All the assumptions and expectations of everyone in a culture flow together and make one big cultural prayer-field.

"The general level any culture achieves is determined almost solely by how conscious its members are about, first, the existence of their prayer-fields in general, and then second, how to extend them consciously. When the extensions are finally practiced, the energy level soars. If everyone in the outer cultures knew how to bring in energy and flow it out, making the prayer extensions a priority, they could achieve the level we have here at Shambhala just like that!" She snapped her fingers for emphasis, then added. "That's what we are working on at the temples. We use our prayer extensions to help raise the awareness in the outer cultures. We've done this for thousands of years."

I considered her words, then asked, "Tell me everything you know about the Fourth Extension."

She was silent a moment longer, staring at me very seriously.

"You know you must take it one step at a time," she replied. "You were helped, but in order to get here you had to know the first three extensions and part of the Fourth. You must stop now and understand exactly how the extensions actually work.

"When an extension is completed, one's energy reaches out farther and becomes stronger. This occurs because when you send your energy out to bring in synchronistic experiences and uplift others, and when you anchor this energy with detachment and faith, you are promoting the divine plan, and the more you can act and think in harmony with the divine, the stronger your power gets. Do you see? There is a built-in safety device, as you've no doubt seen. God is not going to turn up the power in you unless you are on the same page with universal intention."

She touched my shoulder. "So what you have to do now is get clearer about where humanity is supposed to go, how overall human culture must evolve. It is time for this to happen. That is why you and others are finally seeing and understanding Shambhala. This is the next step in the Fourth Extension. You must really grasp the intended future of humanity.

"Already you've grasped how we have mastered technology and placed it in the service of our inner spiritual evolution. Experiencing this extends your energy out farther because you can now set this expectation into your prayer-field.

"It is important to understand how this works. You already know how to send a field out in front of you as you walk through this world, and you know how to set it to increase energy and synchronistic flow in yourself and others. You extend your field another step when you not only visualize your field uplifting the people around you into their higher intuitions but do it with a certainty of where everyone's higher intuitions, yours and theirs, are leading: toward an ideal spiritual culture like the one you see here in Shambhala. When you do this, it helps them find their part to play in this evolution."

I nodded, anxious for more information.

"Don't go too fast," she cautioned. "You have not yet seen all of how we live here. Not only have we mastered technology, we have also restructured our world to focus entirely on spiritual evolution . . . on the mysteries of existence . . . on the life process itself."

8

THE LIFE PROCESS

I took a left fork in the walking trail behind Ani and Tashi's house and made my way up through the rocks and trees for almost a mile. Ani had ended our conversation abruptly, saying that she had to make some preparations that she would tell me about later, and I had decided to take a walk by myself.

As I gazed out on the green foliage, questions filled my mind. Ani had said I needed to see how Shambhala modeled a culture focused on the life process. What did that mean?

As I pondered the question, I noticed a man walking toward me on the path. He was older, appearing to be about fifty, walking at a brisk pace. When he reached me, his eyes lingered on mine for a moment and then he walked on by. Out of the corner of my eye, I saw him turn once and look back at me.

I walked a bit farther, irritated that I hadn't stopped and started a conversation. I turned around and headed back in the direction the man had been walking, hoping I could catch up with him. He was just rounding a corner up ahead and moving out of sight. When I got to the corner myself, he had disappeared altogether. I was disappointed but walked back to Ani's house without thinking any more about it.

She greeted me at the door with some jeans and a shirt.

"You'll need these," she said.

"Let me guess," I said. "You used your field to create these."

She nodded. "You're beginning to understand us."

I sat down in a chair and looked at her. I didn't feel as though I understood at all.

"Tashi's father has arrived," she said.

"Where is he?" I asked.

"In with Tashi." She nodded toward a bedroom.

"Where did he come from?"

"He's been at the temples for a while."

I perked up. "Did he just come in?"

"Yes, just before you came back."

"I think I passed him just now on the path."

Ani paused, then said, "I think he is here to prepare us."

"For what?"

"For the transition. He thinks we are nearing the time when Shambhala will move."

I was about to ask her more when I noticed she had looked away, appearing to be in deep thought.

"You said you saw Tashi's father on the path?" she asked.

I nodded.

"Then the message he is bringing must be important for you too. We have to be very conscious of the process here."

She looked at me expectantly.

"You mentioned the life process," I said. "Can you tell me exactly what those in Shambhala understand that to be?"

She nodded. "Let's look at the whole picture of how a society can evolve once it begins to raise its level of prayer-energy. The first thing that happens is that those who create the technology will begin to make it ever more efficient and automated, so that robots make more and more of the material goods in the society. This is already occurring in every industry in the outer cultures and is a positive development, despite the fact that it is especially dangerous. It can place too much power in the hands of a few individuals or corporations unless it is decentralized. It also creates job losses, and many people have to adjust how they make a living.

"What mediates these problems, however, is the fact that, as material production is automated, the overall economy will begin to shift toward one of information and service—providing just the right information at just the right time for others—which will necessitate everyone becoming more intuitive and alert and focused on synchronistic perception as a way of life.

"As spiritual knowledge increases, and people become aware of the creative power they can attain with their prayer-fields, technology is evolved another step. That's when the thought wave amplifiers will be discovered so that individuals can create everything they need mentally.

"When this happens, the culture will be free to focus completely on spiritual matters, or what we call the life process itself. This is where we are now in Shambhala and where the rest of human culture is destined to follow. Our whole society is educated to the wider reality of the spirit. At some point every culture must truly grasp that we are spiritual beings and that our bodies themselves are only atoms in a particular vibration, a vibration that can be raised as our connection and prayer power increase.

"Here in Shambhala we understand that fact, and we also understand that we come down here from the purely spiritual plane to accomplish something. We come here on a mission to bring the whole world into full spiritual awareness, generation by generation, and to do it as consciously as possible. That's why we participate fully in this life process from the very beginning—before birth itself, in fact."

She looked at me to see if I understood, then continued. "There is always an intuitive relationship between the mother and father and the unborn child before birth."

"What kind of relationship?" I asked.

She smiled. "Everyone here knows that souls begin to contact parents before conception. They make their presence known, especially with the mother. It's part of the process of deciding whether the prospective parent is actually the right one."

I looked at her with astonishment.

"This already occurs in the outer cultures," Ani explained. "It's just that people are only now beginning to talk about it and to develop their perception. Ask any group of mothers and see what they say.

"This same kind of intuition is involved in the marriage process as well, if you think about it. As humans learn to seek out a mate consciously, the main measure is passion, but that's not the only factor. We also get intuitions of what life will look like with a particular person. We assess—whether we are fully conscious of it or not—if the style of life with that individual will represent an advance forward from the style and attitudes we ourselves grew up with.

"Do you see what I'm getting at? Choosing the right mate is important from an evolutionary point of view. As we evolve spiritually, humans are destined to mate consciously in order to set up a home, or home attitude, that represents a more truthful way of life compared to the previous generation. Intuitively we know that we must build a life that adds to the wisdom we found in the world when we arrived. See the process?

"Then, when intuitions come in about a child who wants to

be born to us, they always bring up questions: Why would this child want to be born to our family? What would this child want to be when he or she grows up? How would this child stretch and expand the understanding he or she found with us?"

"Wait a minute," I said. "Don't we have to be careful in assuming we know how our kids will turn out? What if we're wrong and we try to fit our children into some pigeonhole that isn't best for them? My mother thought I was going to be a country preacher, and that wasn't accurate."

"Yes, of course, these are only intuitions; the reality will only be close to what we think. It will never be exact. Centuries were spent arranging marriages and forcing children to enter professions chosen by the parents. But don't you see? This was the misuse of a real intuition. We can learn from what they did wrong. We don't receive final knowledge about our children, nor should we exercise total control. We merely receive intuitions, broad images of what they are going to do with their lives—although I'd bet your mother wasn't far wrong about you."

I laughed. She was right, of course.

"So, you can see where all this is leading. We know that while the mother and father are intuiting how the child will use the wisdom the child will find with them, and then stretch it further, the unborn soul is doing the same thing in a pre-life vision of what it wants to accomplish. Next comes the conception process."

She looked at me for a moment. "Do you remember the couple we saw at the waterfall?"

"Yes."

"What do you think about that?"

"It seemed to be very deliberate."

"That's right, it was. Once a couple decides to attempt conception to bring in a soul they intuit, the physical act is a kind of merging of energy fields that in a very real way orgasmically opens a gate into heaven and allows the soul in."

I thought about what I had seen at the waterfall. The couple's energy merged and a new energy began to grow.

"In the materialistic mind-set of science in the outer cultures," she went on, "the sexual union has been reduced to mere biology, just a physical act. But here we know the spiritual energy of what is really going on. The two merged their energy fields into one and the child was a product of the merger.

"Again, science prefers to think of conception as a random combining of genes, and certainly it looks like that when superficially studied in a test tube. In actuality, however, the genes of the mother and father combine to make a child whose characteristics are synchronistic with the best destinies of all three people. Do you see? The child has an intended destiny that he or she visualizes in a pre-life vision, and the genes combine in a precise way to give the child the tendencies and talents needed to fulfill this vision. Scientists in the outer cultures will eventually find a way to confirm this process.

"That's why the physical recombining of genes by scientists and doctors is so dangerous. Helping to combat disease is one thing, but recombining to increase intelligence or talent or just because of preference comes from the ego and can be disastrous. This practice alone led to the destruction of some early civilizations.

"My point," she concluded, "is that here in Shambhala we take the parenting process very seriously. In its ideal form, the parents' intuition and the child's intuition work together to give the child the best preparation for accomplishing his or her life purpose."

What she was saying made me think again of the missing conceptions occurring in Shambhala.

"What do you think is happening to conceptions that have been disappearing here?" I asked.

She shrugged, glancing at the closed door of Tashi's room. "I don't know, but perhaps we will find out from Tashi's father."

Another question came to mind, so I asked, "I don't understand who goes to the temples and who stays in the rings."

She laughed. "I suppose it is quite confusing. Our culture is divided into those who teach and those who are called to the temples. Many of those who are at the temples, though, come back and forth every few days to maintain relationships, especially if they have children. The situation can change at any time, based on intuition. Those who work at the temples can come back to teach, and those who have been teaching will go to the temples. It is all very fluid and synchronistic."

She paused for a moment and I nodded for her to continue.

"Next in the life process is helping a child to wake up. Remember, each of us forgets to some degree why we came, what we intended to do with our lives, so the child must be given the historical circumstances that surround the event of his birth.

"What's important is to give the child a context for life so that he knows what has occurred before he arrived and where he fits in. That includes the personal history of his family, back several generations. These we keep on a recorder similar to a videotape, except that it is stored electronically.

"Tashi, for instance, was able to watch his relatives back seven generations telling him about their lives, what their dreams had been, what worked and didn't work, and at the end of their lives, what they would have done differently. All this is immensely important information for a youngster to hear from relatives. It helps younger people chart the course of their own lives by learning from the mistakes and building on the wisdom of those who came before. Tashi has learned much from many of his ancestors, although his favorite relative is still his grandmother."

I was amazed. "Recording relatives is a great idea. I wonder why we don't take the time to do this back home."

"You don't take the time because you still postpone talking about death until the very last minute, and then often it's too late. And life in the outer cultures is still focused too much on the material, not on the life process itself. This will become easier as time goes by and the outer cultures begin to sustain their vibrancy and learn the prayer extensions. Right now you still reduce life to the ordinary, to the mundane, when in fact it is a constantly mysterious, informative process."

She looked at me as though there was some deeper meaning behind her last statement.

"You yourself have to overcome this tendency and stay focused on the process of what is happening to you. You have reached Shambhala at a time when it is going into transition. Tashi's father is here to talk to Tashi about his future and the situation at the temples. Yet Tashi doesn't feel intuitively led to go to the temples. Instead he's interested in going to your world. And you show up right in the middle of this. It all means something."

As though to punctuate what Ani had just said, we both heard a faint roaring sound in the distance, which quickly disappeared.

She looked confused. "That's nothing I've ever heard before."

A chill went through me. "I think it might be a helicopter," I said.

Again I thought about telling her about my dream, but before I could she began talking again.

"We have to hurry," she said. "You have to know who we are, the culture we've created. We were talking about the importance of young people understanding the sequence of generations that came before them. This history is something that all individuals in the outer rings become aware of at an early age—as they wake up to their own spirituality and sense of what they came here to do."

She raised her finger. "Everyone here is clear that the human world evolves through the succession of generations. One generation establishes a way of life and meets certain challenges, and the next generation comes along and extends that worldview. Unfortunately in the outer cultures this evolution is just beginning to be taken seriously. More frequently what occurs is that parents want children to be just like them, to take the same view of everything. This desire is natural in a way because we all want our children to reinforce the choices we have made.

"But often the process becomes antagonistic. The parents criticize the interests of the children, and the children criticize the old-fashioned ways of the parents. To some degree it is part of the process: Children look at the lives of the parents and think, I like most of how they live, but I would have done certain things differently. All children have a sense of what is incomplete in their parents' way of life. After all, that's the system: We chose our parents in part to be awakened to what is missing, to what needs to be added to human understanding, and we begin that process by being dissatisfied with what we find in our lives with them.

"Yet all of this doesn't have to be antagonistic. Once we know the life process, we can participate consciously. Parents can be open to the criticisms of their children, and be supportive of their dreams. Of course, doing this causes the parents to have to stretch their own ways of thinking and evolve along with their children, which can be difficult."

I had heard that before. She was going out of her way to make the process of evolution very clear to me. I asked a few more questions, and she spent another ten minutes giving me the details of life in the outer rings of Shambhala. She explained that once children gained an understanding of history and family, the next step for them was to learn to extend their creative prayer field, just as I had. They then went on to find a way to advance the culture, either teaching in the outer rings or using their prayer-field at the temples.

"This will eventually be the lifestyle in the outer cultures as well," she added. "Some will be devoted to the teaching of children, and others will enter the many institutions of human culture and help move them toward the spiritual ideal."

I was about to ask more about what they did at the temples when the door to Tashi's room swung open. Tashi came out, followed by his father.

"Father wants to see you," Tashi said, looking at me. The older man bowed slightly and Tashi introduced us, then both sat down at the table. Tashi's father was dressed in the traditional sheepskin pants and vest of a Tibetan herdsman, except that his clothing was immaculately clean and a light tan color. He was short and stocky and looked at me with kind eyes and an expression of boyish enthusiasm.

"You know that Shambhala is about to go into transition?" he asked.

I looked at Ani and then back at him. "Only what some of the legends say."

"The legends say," the older man replied, "that at a precise time in the evolution of Shambhala and the outer cultures, a great shift will occur. This shift can only happen when the level of awareness in the outer cultures has reached a particular point. But when it does, Shambhala will move."

"Move where?" I asked. "Do you know?"

He smiled. "No one knows exactly."

His statement filled me with a wave of anxiety for some reason, and a slight dizziness. For a moment I had a hard time focusing my eyes.

"He's still not that strong yet." Ani said.

Tashi's father looked at me. "I'm here because of my intuition that it is important that Tashi join us at the temples during this transition. The legends say it will be a time of great opportunity but also of dire peril. For a time what we have been doing here in the temples will be disrupted. We will not be able to help as much."

He looked over at his son. "This will happen just as the situation in the outer cultures becomes critical. Many times during the hidden history of mankind, humans have developed spiritually to this point and then have lost their way and fallen back into ignorance. They began to misuse their technology, disrupting the natural course of evolution.

"For instance, right now in the outer cultures, some people are taking the natural process of food and distorting it by genetically manipulating seeds to have unnatural characteristics. This is primarily done in order to patent these seeds and control them in the marketplace.

"The same thing is occurring in the pharmaceutical industries, where a known herbal remedy, free to all, is genetically altered in order to sell it. In the precise energy system of the body, these manipulations can have terrible consequences on health. The same is true of irradiated foods, chlorine and other additives to the water supply, not to mention so-called designer drugs.

"At the same time, the technology of the media has reached a point where it can have dramatic influence. If it responds only to the needs of corporations and corrupt politicians, it can create realities for humans that are distorted and unnatural. As corporations merge, so that they control more and more of the technology and want to use more advertising to create false needs, this problem will grow.

"Most imperative is the situation of government power and surveillance, even in the democratic countries. Citing a need to combat drug dealers or terrorists, the government has infringed more and more on the privacy of the common man. Already, cash transactions are being restricted and the Internet fully monitored. The next step will be forcing the move to a cashless society controlled by a central authority.

"This growth toward a central, spiritless governmental authority, in a high-tech virtual world divorced from natural processes, where food, water, and the routines of living have been trivialized and distorted, leads to disaster. When health is subverted into just one more commercial cycle of worsening food, new diseases, and more drugs, Armageddon is the result, and it has occurred several times in prehistory. It could happen again, only this time on a much larger scale."

He smiled over at Ani. "But it need not happen. In fact, we are one small step in awareness from turning the corner. If we could just move fully into the idea that we are spiritual beings in a spiritual world, then food, health, technology, media, and government would all move into their proper roles in the evolution and perfection of this world. But for this to happen, the prayer extensions must be completely understood in the outer cultures. They must understand what we do at the temples. The transition of Shambhala is part of this process, but the opportunity has to be seized."

He looked deeply at Tashi. "For this to happen your generation must merge with the last two into an integrated prayer-field—one that includes a final unity of all the religions."

Tashi looked confused, and his father moved closer to him.

"All over the world, the generation born in the first decades of the twentieth century, what our friend from the West would call the World War II generation, used courage and technology to save democracy and freedom from the threat of dictators seeking empire. They won, using technological might, and continued to expand this technology into a worldwide economy. Then the next generation—what Americans call baby boomers—arrived on the Earth, and their intuitions told them that the focus on materialism, on technology alone, was not quite correct. That there was too much pollution, too much corporate influence on government, too much surveillance by the intelligence organizations.

"This criticism was the normal way that a new generation expands and intuitively leads us forward. They grew up in a hard-won materialism, or in some countries, the desire for the material, and began to react, to voice the idea that there was more to life. There was a spiritual purpose behind human history that could be grasped in more detail.

"That's what was behind all that happened in the sixties and seventies in the West: the rejection of a material-based system of status, the exploration of other religions, the popularity of philosophy, the explosion in thought of the Human Potential Movement. It was all the result of a series of insights that there was more to life than our material worldview knew."

He regarded me with a twinkle, as though he knew everything about my experiences with the Insights.

"The intuitions of the baby boomers were very important," he went on, "because they began to put technology and material abundance into perspective, and to grasp the deep intuition that technology is being developed on this planet to support a culture where we can focus not just on surviving, but on our spiritual development as well."

He paused for a moment. "And now, since the late seventies and into the eighties, a new generation has been arriving to push human culture even further." He looked at Tashi. "You and your age group are the final members of this generation. Do you see what emphasis you are bringing into the world?"

As Tashi pondered the inquiry, I thought about the question myself. The sons and daughters of the boomers have been characterized as reacting to the boomers' idealism and ambivalence toward technology by becoming more practical and, in fact, developing a love for technology beyond anything seen before.

Everyone looked at me as though they had heard my thoughts. Tashi was nodding in agreement.

"We sensed that technology has a spiritual purpose," he said.

"Now," the older Tibetan continued, looking at all of us, "do you see how the three generations flow together? The World War II generation fought against tyranny and proved that democracy could not only flourish in the modern world but expand tremendously and connect the world's economies. Then, in the middle of the abundance, the boomers arrived to say that there were problems with this expansion, that we were polluting the natural world and losing touch with nature and a spiritual reality that exists beneath the whims of history.

"And now the next generation has come along to focus again on the economy, to refashion technology so that it can consciously support our mental and spiritual ability, the way it has occurred here in Shambhala—instead of allowing technology to fall solely into the hands of those who would use it to restrict freedom and control others."

"But this new generation isn't fully conscious of what they are doing," I said.

"No, not completely," he replied. "But this self-awareness and insight is expanding every day. We must set a prayer-field that lifts them in this direction. It must be a large and strong field. The new generation must help us unify the religions.

"This is very important, because there will always be control-lers ready to manipulate this generation into creating negative uses for technology or taking advantage of their alienation."

As we sat there, we all heard the low drone of helicopters again, still far in the distance.

"The transition is beginning," Tashi's father said, looking at him. "There are many preparations to make. I wanted only to convey that the generation you represent must now help push all of us forward. You personally have some role in expanding into the outer cultures what Shambhala has been doing. But only you can decide what you must do."

The young man looked away.

His father went over and put his arm around him for a mo-ment. Then he embraced Ani and left the house.

Tashi followed him with his eyes as he walked through the door and returned alone to his room.

I followed Ani out into a sitting area in the garden, full of ques-tions.

"Where did Tashi's father go?" I asked.

"He's getting ready for the transition," she replied, glancing back at me. "This may not be easy. We may all be displaced for a while. There are many who are coming back from the temples and helping."

I shook my head. "What do you think will happen?"

"No one knows," she replied. "The legends are not specific. All we know is that there will be a transition."

The uncertainty began to diminish my energy level again, and I sat down on one of the benches nearby.

Ani followed and sat beside me. "I do know what you must

do," she said. "You must continue to pursue the rest of the Fourth Extension. Everything else will take care of itself."

I nodded halfheartedly.

"Focus on what you have learned here. You have seen how technology must evolve, and you have now begun to see how our culture focuses itself on the life process, the miracle of birth and conscious evolution. You know that this is the focus that creates the most inspiration and the most fun.

"The materialistic life in the outer cultures pales when compared to it. We are spiritual beings, and our lives must revolve around the mysteries of family and talent and the search for individual mission. Again, you now know what such a culture looks and feels like.

"The legends say that knowing with certainty how cultures can evolve extends everyone's prayer-field and gives it more power. Now when you connect within and see your field flowing out in front of you, acting to bring synchronicity and uplifting others into the synchronistic process, you can do so with greater expectation, because you know with certainty where this process is taking us all, if we stay true to it and avoid fear and hate."

She was right. The extensions were all falling into place.

"But I haven't seen it all," I said.

"She looked deeply into my eyes. "No, you must continue to understand the rest of the Fourth Extension. There is more. Your prayer-field can become more powerful yet."

At that moment we could hear the helicopters again, and the sound of them filled me with anger. They seemed to be getting closer. How was this possible? How could they know where Shambhala was?

"Damn them," I said, which produced a horrified look on Ani's face.

"You have much anger," she said.

"Well, it's hard not to be angry when you realize what the Chinese military is doing."

"This anger is a pattern in you. I'm sure you have been warned of its effect."

I thought back to all Yin had tried to explain. "Yes, I have. I just keep messing up."

I could tell she was concerned.

"You'll have to master this problem," she said. "But don't get down on yourself too much. That sends out a negative prayer that keeps you where you are. On the other hand, you can't just ignore your anger. You must keep the problem in mind, remind yourself, stay conscious, and at the same time set your prayer-field that you will break through and discard the old pattern."

I knew that was a very fine line to walk and would take conscious work on my part.

"What should I do now?" I asked.

"What do you think?"

"I've got to go to the temples?"

"Is that your intuition?"

I thought again about my dream and finally told her about it. Her eyes grew wide.

"You dreamed of going to the temples with Tashi?" she asked.

"Yeah," I replied.

"Well," she said sternly, "don't you think you should tell him about it?"

I walked up to Tashi's room and touched the wall.

"Come in," he said, and an opening appeared.

Tashi was stretched out on his bed. He immediately sat up and gestured to a chair across from him. I sat down.

For a moment he was silent, the weight of the world on his shoulders. Finally he said, "I still don't know what to do."

"What are you thinking?" I asked.

"I don't know, I'm confused. All I can think of is getting to the outer cultures. My mother says I must find my own way. I wish my grandmother was here."

"Where is your grandmother?"

"She's at the temples somewhere."

We stared at each other for a long time and then he added, "If only I could understand this dream I had."

I sat up straight. "What dream?"

"I'm with another group of people. I can't see their faces, but I know that one of them is my sister." He paused for a moment. "I could also see a place with water. Somehow I'd gotten to the outer cultures."

"I've had a dream too," I said. "You were with me. We were at one of the temples . . . it was blue . . . and we found someone else there."

A trace of a smile crossed Tashi's face.

"What are you saying?" he asked. "That I'm supposed to go to the temples instead of to the outer cultures?"

"No," I said. "That's not what I mean. You told me that everyone thinks it's impossible to get to the outer cultures through the temples. But what if it's not?"

His face lit up. "You mean, go to the temples and try to get to the outer cultures from there?"

I just looked at him.

"That must be it," he said, standing up. "Perhaps I have been called, after all."

9

THE ENERGY OF EVIL

No sooner had we walked out of the bedroom than the sounds of the helicopters in the distance increased.

Ani came into the house and pulled out three heavy backpacks from a storage bin. She handed them to us along with two parkas. I noticed that they seemed to have been conventionally made with cloth and stitching. I was about to ask about them, but she quickly ushered us out of the dwelling and led us down the path to our left.

As we walked, Ani moved up beside Tashi and I could hear him telling her about his decision to go to the temples. The rumblings from the helicopters were coming ever closer, and the blue sky had now turned into a thick overcast.

At one point I asked her where we were heading.

"To the caves," she said. "You'll need some time to prepare."

We walked down a rocky path which traversed the side of a sheer cliff and onto a plateau on the other side. Here Ani waved us into a small gully, where we huddled, listening. The helicopters moved in a small circle over the cliffs for a moment and followed our path exactly until they were directly over us.

Ani looked horrified.

"What's happening?" I yelled.

Without answering she climbed out of the gully and motioned for us to follow. We ran perhaps half a mile across the plateau and into another hilly area, then stopped and waited. As before, the helicopters circled behind us until they arrived directly overhead.

A gust of frigid air hit us, almost knocking me over. At the same time, all of the clothes disappeared from our bodies except for the heavy coats.

"I thought this might happen," Ani said, pulling more clothes from the packs. I still had my boots on, but Tashi's and Ani's had disappeared. She gave him a pair made of leather and put on another herself. When we finished, we made our way up the slope, climbing between the rocks until we arrived at a flatter area. A heavy snow shower was beginning and the temperature was falling. The helicopters seemed to have lost their way for the moment.

I looked out on the once green valley. Snow had covered almost everything and the plants already seemed to be withering from the cold.

"It's the effect of the soldiers' energy," Ani said. "It is destroying our environmental field."

Glancing toward the sound of the helicopters, I felt a new surge of anger. They banked immediately and headed straight toward us.

"Let's go," Ani shouted.

I moved up closer to the small fire, feeling the morning chill. We had walked for another hour and spent the night in a small cave. In spite of several layers of insulated undergarments, I was still freezing. Tashi was now huddled up beside me, and Ani was looking out through the opening at the frozen world outside. The snow had been falling for hours.

"It's all gone now," Ani said. "There's nothing out there now but ice."

I moved over to the opening and looked out. What was once a wooded valley with hundreds of dwellings was now nothing but snow and jagged mountains. Here and there were the bent-over remains of trees, but not a spot of color could be seen. All the houses had simply vanished, and the river that ran through the center of the valley was frozen over.

"The temperature must have fallen sixty degrees," Ani added.

"What happened?" I asked.

"When the Chinese found us, the power of their thoughts and their expectations of frigid weather counteracted the field that we had set to keep the temperature moderate. Ordinarily the strength of the fields provided by those at the temples would have been strong enough to have kept the Chinese away altogether, but they knew it was time for the transition."

"What? They let them in on purpose?"

"It was the only way. If you and the others who have found us were allowed in, there was no way to keep out the soldiers. You are not strong enough to keep all negative thoughts out of your mind. And the Chinese have followed you here."

"You mean this is my fault?" I said.

"It's okay. It is part of the dispersal."

I wasn't consoled. I moved back to the fire and Ani followed. Tashi had prepared a stew of dried vegetables.

"You must realize," she said, "that everything is all right with the people of Shambhala. All this was expected. Everyone who was here is fine. Enough people came back from the temples to take them through the spatial windows to a new place of safety. Our legends have prepared us well."

She pointed out toward the valley. "You must focus on what you're doing. You and Tashi have to make it to the temples without being captured by the military. The rest of what Shambhala has been doing for humanity must be known."

She stopped as we both heard the faint rumblings of a distant helicopter. The sound grew fainter and finally disappeared.

"And you must be much more careful," she said. "I thought you knew not to allow negative images into your mind, especially hateful or disparaging thoughts."

I knew she was right, but I still felt confused about how all that worked.

She looked hard at me. "Sooner or later, you're going to have to deal with your pattern of anger."

I was about to ask a question when out through the cave opening we saw several dozen people walking down an icy slope to our right.

Ani stood up and looked at Tashi.

"There is no more time," she said. "I have to go. I have to help these people find a way out. Your father will be waiting on me."

"Can't you come with us?" Tashi asked, moving closer to her.

I could see that he had tears in his eyes.

Ani stared at him and looked out the icy crevice at the other people.

"I can't," she said, hugging him tightly. "My place is here, helping with the transition. But don't worry. I'll find you wherever you are."

She walked toward the mouth of the cave and turned around to face both of us.

"You will be fine," she said. "But be careful. You cannot keep your energy up if you are overwhelmed with anger. You must have no enemies."

She stopped and looked at me, and then said something I had heard many times on this journey.

"And remember," she instructed, smiling, "you are being helped."

Tashi looked over his shoulder and smiled at me as we trudged through the deep snow. It was getting colder, and I struggled to maintain my energy. To reach the mountain range holding the temples, we had to climb down the ridge we were on, cross the frozen valley, and climb almost straight up and over another mountain. We had made our way down almost a quarter of a mile without difficulty but now seemed to be reaching the edge of a rock precipice. Below was a sheer drop-off of almost fifty feet.

Tashi turned and looked at me. "We'll have to slide down it. There's no way around."

"That's too dangerous," I protested. "There might be rocks just under the snow. If we start sliding out of control, we could be hurt." My energy was plummeting.

Tashi smiled nervously. "It's okay," he said. "It's okay to be afraid. Just maintain your visualization of a positive outcome. Fear will actually bring the dakini closer."

"Wait a minute," I said. "No one ever mentioned that before. What do you mean?"

"Haven't you been helped mysteriously, inexplicably?"

"Yin told me Shambhala was helping me."

"Well?"

"I don't understand the relationship. I've been trying to find out what determines when the dakini help us."

"Only those in the temples know that. I just know that fear

always brings these guardians closer, if we can still maintain our faith to some degree. It is hate that drives them away."

Tashi pulled me forward off the ledge, and we began to slide in the loose snow uncontrollably. My foot hit a rock and flipped me over, and I began rolling head over heels. I knew if my head hit another rock, it could be all over. But in spite of the fear, I managed to hold a vision of landing safely.

With that thought, a particular feeling began to come over me, and I was filled with a sense of peace and well-being. The terror subsided. Moments later I hit the bottom of the drop-off and rolled to a stop. Tashi slammed into my back. I lay for a moment with my eyes closed. I opened them slowly, remembering other dangerous situations in my life when an inexplicable peace had come over me.

Tashi was pulling himself out of the snowbank, and I smiled over at him.

"What?" he asked.

"Someone was here."

Tashi stood up and shook the snow off his clothes and began to walk on. "You see what happens when you stay positive? Whatever temporary strength comes from anger cannot compare with this mystery."

I nodded, hoping I could remember that.

For two hours we made our way across the valley floor, crossing the frozen river and working our way up the gradual slope to the base of the steep mountains. The snow was beginning to fall harder.

Suddenly Tashi stopped.

"Something moved up ahead," he said.

I strained to see. "What was it?"

"It looked like a person. Come on."

We proceeded up the slope of the mountain. Its peak looked to be about two thousand feet above us.

"There has to be a pass somewhere," Tashi said. "We can't go over the top."

Ahead of us we heard the sound of sliding snow and rocks. Tashi and I glanced at each other and moved slowly around a series of large outcroppings. As we made our way past the last one, we could see a man shaking himself out of the snow. He looked exhausted. A bloody bandage was wrapped around one of his knees. I couldn't believe my eyes. It was Wil.

"It's okay," I said to Tashi. "I know this man." I stood up and crawled over the rocks.

Wil heard us and dived to the side, ready in spite of his leg to run down a narrow draw away from us.

"It's me," I called to him.

Wil stood up tall for a moment, then collapsed again in the snow. He was dressed in a thick white parka and insulated pants.

"It's about time," he said, smiling. "I was expecting you earlier."

Tashi rushed over and looked at Wil's leg. I introduced them. As quickly as I could, I explained to Wil everything that had happened to me: meeting Yin, fleeing the Chinese, learning the extensions, getting through the gateway, and finally reaching the rings of Shambhala.

"I didn't know how to find you," I added, pointing down to the valley. "Everything's been ruined. It's the effect of the Chinese."

"I know," Wil said. "I've already run into them myself."

Wil went on to tell us about his experiences. Like me, he had extended his prayer-field the best he could and been allowed into

Shambhala. He'd been in another part of the rings, where he was educated further in the legends by another family.

"The temples are very difficult to reach," Wil said. "Especially now with the Chinese soldiers coming. We must make sure we are not engaging in negative prayer."

"I don't seem to be doing so well in that area," I replied.

He looked at me sharply, concerned. "But that's why you were with Yin. Didn't he show you what can happen?"

"I think I understand how to avoid the general fear images. It's my anger against the Chinese soldiers that keeps slipping me up."

Wil looked even more alarmed and was about to say something when we heard the sounds of helicopters closing in the distance. We began our climb up the mountain, weaving our way through the rocks and deep snowbanks. Everything seemed to be very fragile and unstable. We climbed for another twenty minutes without talking. The wind was increasing now, and the snow stung against our faces.

Wil stopped and dropped to one knee.

"Listen," he said. "What's that?"

"It's the helicopter again," I said, fighting my irritation.

As we listened, the helicopter sliced through the overhanging clouds and began to fly straight toward us.

Limping slightly, Wil made his way farther up the icy slope, but I paused for an instant, hearing something else above the noise of the helicopter. It sounded like a freight train.

"Look out!" Wil screamed from ahead of me. "It's an avalanche."

I tried to run out of the way, but it was too late. The full force of the rolling snow hit me in the face and knocked me backward down the slope. I was tumbling and sliding, sometimes covered completely by the weight of the thundering avalanche, sometimes riding on the surface of the moving mass.

After what seemed like forever, I felt myself come to a stop. I was packed in, unable to move, my body in a contorted position under the snow. I tried to suck in a breath, but there was no air. I knew I was about to die.

But someone grabbed my outstretched right arm and began to dig me out. I could feel others digging around me, and finally my head was free. I gasped for air, wiping the snow from my eyes, expecting to see Wil.

Instead I saw a dozen Chinese soldiers, one of them still holding my arm. In the background walking toward me was Colonel Chang. Without talking, he signaled several of the other soldiers to take me to a hovering helicopter. A rope ladder was dropped, and some of the soldiers swiftly climbed aboard, then threw down a harness, which was placed around me. The colonel gave the order, and I was hauled aboard as he and the remaining soldiers climbed in. In minutes we were flying away.

I stood looking out a porthole-sized window of a thirty-by-thirty-foot insulated tent. Altogether I could count at least seven large tents and three small, portable trailers of a size that could be airlifted easily. A gasoline generator hummed at the corner of the compound, and I could see several helicopters sitting in an area to the left. The snow had stopped falling but had accumulated twelve or fourteen inches on the ground.

I strained to see to the right. From the lay of the mountain range in the background I concluded that I had been flown only as far back as the center of the valley. A nighttime wind howled, flapping the outside seams of the tent.

When I had arrived, I had been fed, forced to take a lukewarm shower, and given warm Chinese fatigues and insulated underwear to put on. At least I was finally warm.

I turned around and looked over at the armed Chinese guard sitting at the entrance. His eyes had been following my every move with a cold, icy stare that chilled my soul. Fatigued, I walked over and sat down on one of two army cots in the corner. I tried to assess my situation but I couldn't think. I was numb, petrified, so fearful, in fact, that I knew I wasn't very alert. I couldn't understand why I felt so incapacitated. It was a panic as intense as any I had ever experienced.

I tried to take a deep breath and build energy, but I couldn't even get started. The bare lightbulbs hanging from the tent's ceiling filled the room with a dull, flickering light and ominous shadows. I could find no beauty anywhere around me.

The flap of the tent opened up and the soldier stood up at attention. Colonel Chang walked in and took off his thick parka, nodding to the guard. He then focused on me. I looked away.

"We must talk," he said, pulling a folding chair over and sitting four feet away. "I must have the answers to my questions. Now." He stared at me coldly for a moment. "Why are you here?"

I decided to answer as truthfully as I could. "I'm here studying Tibetan legend. I told you that."

"You're here looking for Shambhala."

I was silent.

"Is that it?" he asked. "Is it in this valley?"

The fear churned in my stomach. What would he do if I refused to answer?

"Don't you know?" I asked.

He smiled slightly. "I would guess that you and the rest of your illegal sect think this is Shambhala." He looked puzzled, as though remembering something else. "We've glimpsed other people here. But they have managed to elude us in the snow. Where are they? Where did they go?"

"I don't know," I said. "I don't even know where we are."

He shifted toward me. "We have also found the remains of plants, recently alive. How is that possible? How could they have grown here?"

I just stared.

He grinned coldly. "How much do you really know about the legends of Shambhala?"

"A little," I stammered.

"I know a lot. Do you believe that? By now I've had access to all the ancient writings, and I must say they are delightfully interesting, as mythology. Think about it: an ideal community made up of enlightened human beings that are far more advanced, mentally, than any other culture on this planet.

"And I know the rest too—this idea that these individuals of Shambhala somehow have a secret power for good that permeates all the rest of humanity and pushes them in that direction. Fascinating stuff, don't you think? Ancient lore that could even be appreciated, for that matter . . . if it weren't so misleading and dangerous for the people of Tibet.

"Don't you think if anything like that were real we would have discovered it by now? God, spirit, it's all a childish dream. Take the Tibetan mythology about the dakini, the idea that there are angel beings who can interact with us, help us."

"What do you believe in?" I asked, trying to diffuse the situation.

He pointed to his head. "I believe in the powers of the mind. This is why you should talk to me, help us. We are most interested in the idea of psychic power, the greater range of brain waves and their effect on electronics and people at a distance. But don't confuse this with spiritualism. The powers of mind are a natural phenomenon that can be researched and discovered scientifically."

He ended his statement with an angry gesture with his hand,

sending a deepening pang of fear through my stomach. I knew this man was extremely dangerous and absolutely remorseless.

He was looking at me, but something attracted my attention along the wall of the tent behind him, directly across from the door where the guard was standing. The area had suddenly gotten brighter. The lightbulb overhead flickered slightly, and I dismissed my perception as a surge from the generator.

The colonel got up and walked a few steps toward me, looking more angry. "Do you think I like journeying out here into this wasteland? How anyone survives out here is beyond me. But we are not leaving. We're going to enlarge this camp until we have enough troops to cover this whole area on foot. Whoever is here will be found and dealt with very harshly."

He forced a half-smile. "But our friends will be equally rewarded. Do you understand?"

At this moment another wave of fear rushed through me, but it was different. It was a fear mixed with a great disdain. I was beginning to loathe the extent of this man's evil.

I glanced behind him to the area that seemed lighter, but it was now flat and filled with shadows. The lightness had disappeared, and I felt totally alone.

"Why are you doing this?" I asked. "The Tibetan people have a right to their own religious beliefs. You're trying to destroy their culture. How can you do this?" I could feel my anger making me stronger.

My confrontation seemed only to energize him.

"Oh, you do have opinions," he smirked. "Too bad they are so naive. You think what we are doing is unusual. Your own government is developing ways to control you too. Chips that can be inserted into the body of troops and unsuspecting troublemakers.

"And that's not all." He was almost shouting now. "We know

now that when people think, a specific pattern of brain waves radiates outward. Every government is working on machines that can identify these brain waves, especially angry or antigovernment sentiment."

His statement chilled me. He was talking about the same misuse of brain wave amplification that Ani had warned me about, the one that had doomed some early civilizations to ruin.

"Do you know why your so-called democratic governments are doing this?" he went on. "Because they are far more afraid of the people then we are. Our citizens know the role of government is to govern. They know that certain liberties have to be limited. Your people think there can be individual self-direction. Well, if that was true in the past, in a highly technical world where a suitcase weapon can destroy a city, it cannot work any longer. With that kind of freedom, humans will not survive. The direction, the values, of society must be controlled and directed for the greater good. That's why this Shambhala legend is so dangerous. It is based on absolute self-direction."

As he talked, I thought I heard the door open behind me, but I didn't turn around. I was focused totally on this man's attitude. Here was the worst of modern tyranny being voiced, and the more he talked the more my loathing increased.

"What you don't see," I said, "is that humans can find an inner motivation to create good in the world."

He laughed cynically. "Surely you don't believe that? Nothing in history would suggest that people are anything other than selfish and greedy."

"If you had your own spirituality, you would see the good." My voice was rising in anger too.

"No," he snapped, almost screaming. "Spirituality is the problem. As long as there is religion, there cannot be unity among people. Don't you understand? Each religious institution is like an inflexible roadblock on the path of progress. Each wars with the other. The Christians spend all their time and money wanting to convert everyone into their doctrine of judgmentalness. The Jews want to remain isolated in a dream of chosenness. The Muslims think it's about camaraderie and collective power and holy hatred. And we in the East, we are the worst. We disregard the real world for a fanciful inner life no one can understand. With all this chaos of metaphysics no one can focus on progress, on easing the burden of the poor, on seeing that every Tibetan child is educated.

"But don't worry," he went on. "We're going to see that the problem is resolved. And you have helped us. Ever since Wilson James visited you in America, we've monitored your movements and the movements of the Dutch group. I knew you would come, that you would be involved."

I must have looked surprised.

"Oh yes, we have known all about you. We operate more freely in America than you think. Your NSA can monitor the Internet. Do you think we cannot? You and this sect will never elude me. How do you think we could follow you in this weather? It was by power of mind. My mind. It came to me where you would be. Even after we were lost in this wilderness, I knew. I could feel your presence. At first it was your friend Yin whom I could follow. Now it's been you.

"And that's not all. I don't even need to use my instincts to locate you anymore. I have your brain wave scan." He nodded toward the door. "In a matter of minutes our technicians will have mounted our new surveillance equipment. Then we'll be able to locate anyone we have scanned."

At first I couldn't remember what he was referring to, but then I recalled my experience at the Chinese house in Ali after I was gassed. The soldiers had put me under a machine. A new wave of fear raced through me, but it turned immediately into an even deeper anger.

"You're mad!" I screamed.

"That's right—to you, I'm crazy. But I'm the future." He was towering over me now, his face red, virtually exploding with anger. "Such stupid innocence. You're going to tell me every-thing. You understand! Everything!"

I knew that he would not have given me all this information if he planned to ever release me, but at the moment I didn't care. I was talking to a monster, and an overwhelming rage was filling me. I was about to verbalize his damnation again when a voice from the other side of the room called out.

"Don't! It weakens you!"

The colonel turned and stared, and I followed his gaze. There by the door stood another guard, and beside him, slumping against a small table, was Yin. The guard pushed him to the floor.

I jumped up and raced over to Yin as the colonel said some-thing in Chinese to the guards, then stormed out. Yin had bruises and cuts on his face.

"Yin, are you all right?" I asked, helping him over to a cot.

"I'm okay," he said, pulling me down to sit on the cot beside him. "They came for us right after you left." His eyes were full of excitement. "Tell me what happened. Did you reach Shambhala?"

I looked at him and held my fingers to my lips. "They proba-bly put us together to see what we would say," I whispered. "You can bet they have this place bugged. We shouldn't talk."

"We'll have to risk it," Yin said. "Come over by the heater. It's noisy. Tell me what happened."

For the next half hour I told him all about the world I had found in Shambhala, then, in the barest whisper, I mentioned the temples.

His eyes grew wider. "So you haven't found all of the Fourth Extension?"

I mouthed, "It's at the temples."

I went on to tell him about Tashi and Wil and what Ani had said about learning what those in the temples were doing.

"And what else did she say?" Yin asked.

"She said we must have no enemies," I replied.

Yin grimaced in pain for a moment and then said, "But you are doing exactly that with the colonel. You were using your anger and disdain to feel strong. Those are the mistakes I made. You're lucky he did not kill you immediately."

I slumped back, knowing my emotions were out of control.

"Don't you remember when your negative expectation drove away the Dutch couple in the van, and you missed an important synchronicity? In that case you were having a fear expectation that they were perhaps going to do you harm. They felt that expectation on your part and probably began to feel that if they stopped they would be doing something wrong, so they left."

"Yes, I remember."

"Every negative assumption or expectation," Yin continued, "that we make about another human being is a prayer that goes out and acts to create that reality in that person. Remember our minds connect—our thoughts and expectations go out and influence others to think the same way that we do. That's what you have been doing with the colonel. You have been expecting him to be evil."

"Wait a minute. I was just seeing him the way he is."

"Really? What part of him? His ego or his higher, soul self?"

Yin was right. All this was something I thought I'd learned with the Tenth Insight, but I wasn't acting on it.

"When I was running from him," I said, "he was able to follow me. He said he could do it with his mind and intuition."

"Were you thinking of him?" Yin asked. "Expecting him to follow you?"

"I must have been."

"Don't you remember? That's what was happening with me earlier. And now you are doing the same thing. That expectation was creating the thoughts in Chang's mind of where you were. It was an ego thought, but it came to him because you were expecting—praying, in effect—for him to find you.

"Don't you see?" Yin continued. "We've talked about this so many times. Our prayer-field is working constantly in the world, sending out our expectations, and in the case of another person, the effect is almost instantaneous. Luckily, as I said before, such a negative prayer is not as strong as a positive prayer, because you immediately cut yourself off from your higher-self energies, but it still has an effect. This is the hidden process behind your Golden Rule."

I looked at him for a moment, not understanding. I took a minute to remember what he was referring to: the Bible injunction to do unto others as you would have them do unto you. I couldn't exactly see the connection and asked him to explain.

"The rule sounds," Yin went on, "as though it should be kept because it creates a good society. Right? As an ethical stance. But the fact is there is a real spiritual, energetic, karmic reason that goes beyond the notion that this is a good idea. It is important to keep this rule because you are affected personally."

He paused dramatically, then added, "The more complete expression of this rule should be: Do unto others the way you would have them do unto you because how you treat them or think about them is exactly how they are going to treat you. The prayer that you send out with your feeling or action tends to bring out in them exactly what you expect."

I nodded. This idea was starting to sink in.

"In the case of the colonel, when you conclude he is evil, your prayer-energy goes out and enters his energy and adds to his tendencies. And so he begins to act the way you expect him to act, in an angry, ruthless manner. Because he isn't connected with a deeper divine energy, his ego energy is weak and malleable. He takes on the role you expect of him. Think back to how things generally operate in human culture. This effect is everywhere. Remember that we humans share attitudes and moods. It's all very contagious. When we look out at others and make judgments, thinking that they are fat or thin or underachieved or ugly or poorly dressed, we actually send our energy out at these people and they often begin to think bad thoughts about themselves. We are engaging in what can only be called the energy of evil. It is the contagion of negative prayer."

"But what are we supposed to do?" I protested. "Don't we have to see things as they are?"

"Of course we have to see things the way they are, but after that we must immediately shift our expectations from *what is* to *what could be*. In the case of the colonel, you should have realized that even though he was acting evilly, cut off from anything spiritual, his higher self was capable of seeing the light in an instant. That's the expectation you want to hold, because then you are really sending your prayer-field out to lift his energy and awareness in that direction. You must return to that mental posture, always, no matter what you see."

He paused dramatically, smiling, which I thought was strange, given our situation and his bruised and cut face.

"They beat you?" I asked.

"It's nothing I haven't wished on them," he said, making his point one more time.

"Do you see how important all this is?" Yin asked. "You cannot go further with the extensions until you understand this. Anger will always be a temptation. It feels good. It makes our egos think we are becoming stronger. You have to be smarter than that. You cannot reach the strongest levels of creative energy until you can avoid negative prayer of all kinds. There is enough evil out there without adding to it unconsciously. This is the great truth behind the Tibetan code of compassion."

I looked away, knowing that all Yin was saying was true. I had slipped into this pattern of anger again. Why did I keep doing this over and over?

Yin caught my eye.

"Here is the cap to this idea. In correcting a counterproductive pattern in oneself—in our case, anger and condemnation—it is imperative not to put out a negative prayer about our own possibilities. Do you see what I mean? If we make self-defeating comments such as 'I can't overcome this problem,' or 'I'll always be this way,' then we are in fact praying to stay the way we are. We have to hold a vision that we will find a higher energy and overcome our patterns. We have to uplift ourselves with our own prayer-energy."

He leaned back on the cot. "This is the lesson I myself had to learn. I could never understand the attitude of compassion that Lama Ridgen held toward the Chinese government. They were destroying our country and I wanted them vanquished. I had never been close enough to any of the soldiers to look in their eyes, to see them as people caught up in a tyrannical system.

"But once I saw past their egos, their socialization, I could finally learn not to add to the energy of evil with my negative assumptions. I could finally hold a higher vision for them and myself. Perhaps because I have learned this, I can also hold a higher vision that you will learn it also."

I awoke with the first noise in the camp. Someone was clanking barrels or large cans together. I jumped up, dressed, and glanced toward the door. The guards had been replaced by two other soldiers. They stared at me sleepily. I walked over and looked out the window. The day was dark and overcast and the wind howled. There was movement at one of the other tents; one of the doors was opening. It was the colonel and he was walking toward our tent.

I moved back to Yin's cot and he turned over, struggling to wake up. His face was swollen and he squinted to see me.

"The colonel is coming back," I said.

"I will help as much as I can," he said. "But you will have to hold a different prayer-field for him. It is your only chance."

The flap door tore open and the soldiers jumped to attention. The colonel came in and gestured for them to wait outside. He glanced at Yin once before walking over to me.

I was taking deep breaths and attempting to extend my field as much as possible. I visualized the energy overflowing out from me, and I focused on seeing him not as a torturer, but only as a soul in fear.

"I want to know where these temples are," he said in a low, ominous voice, taking off his coat.

"The only way you can see them is if your energy is high enough," I replied, voicing the first thing that came to my mind.

He seemed to be taken off guard. "What are you talking about?"

"You told me you believe in powers of the mind. What if one of those powers is to raise your energy level?"

"What energy?"

"You said that brain waves were real and could be manipulated by a machine. What if they could be manipulated internally by our intention and made stronger, raising your energy level?"

"How is that possible?" he said. "Nothing like that has ever been shown by science."

I couldn't believe it, he seemed to be opening his mind. I

focused on the expression on his face that seemed to be honestly considering what I was saying.

"But it's really possible," I went on. "Brain waves, or perhaps a different set of waves that go farther, can be increased to a point where we can influence what happens."

He perked up. "Are you telling me you know how to use brain waves to make certain things happen?"

As he talked, I again saw a glow behind him against the wall of the tent.

"Yes," I continued. "But only those things that take our lives in the direction they are supposed to go. Otherwise the energy eventually collapses."

"Supposed to go?" he asked, squinting.

The area of the tent behind him continued to appear lighter and I couldn't help glancing at it. He turned around and looked in that direction himself.

"What are you looking at?" he asked. "Tell me what you mean about 'supposed to go.' I consider myself free. I can take my life anywhere I want."

"Yes, of course, that's true. But there is a direction that feels best, is more inspired, and gives you more satisfaction than all others, isn't there?" I couldn't believe how light the area behind him was becoming, but I dared not look at it directly.

"I don't know what you're talking about," he said.

He looked confused, but I remained focused on the part of his expression that was listening.

"We are free," I said. "But we also belong to a design that comes from a greater part of ourselves that we can connect with. Our true self is much larger than we thought."

He just stared. Somewhere deep in his consciousness, he seemed to be understanding.

We were interrupted when the guards outside banged on the

entrance flap. As they did, I realized that the wind had erupted into a gale. We could hear things being blown and turned over all through the compound.

A guard had opened the flap and was shouting loudly in Chinese. The colonel ran toward him. As he did, we could see tents blowing over everywhere. He turned and looked at Yin and me, and in that moment a tremendous gust of wind blew the left side of our tent up from its foundation and ripped it apart, covering the colonel and guards with canvas, knocking them to the ground.

Yin and I were hit with the wind and snow blowing in through the gaping hole.

"Yin," I shouted. "The dakini."

Yin struggled to his feet. "This is your chance!" he said. "Run."

"Come on," I said, grabbing his arm. "We can go together."

He pushed me away. "I can't. I'll just slow you down."

"We can make it," I pleaded.

He shouted against the howling wind. "I've done what I was here to do. Now you must do the same. We still don't know the rest of the Fourth Extension."

I nodded and embraced him quickly, then grabbed the colonel's heavy coat and ran through the hole in the tent into the storm.

10

ACKNOWLEDGING
THE LIGHT

I ran to the north for about a hundred feet and stopped to look back toward the camp. I could still hear the sounds of debris blowing through the compound, and the din of shouting.

Out ahead of me was a solid sheet of white, and I was trudging back toward the mountains when I heard the colonel yelling.

"I'll find you," he shouted angrily above the wind. "You won't make it."

I walked on, hurrying as much as possible in the deep snow. It took me fifteen minutes to walk a hundred yards. Fortunately the wind was still fierce, and I knew it would be some time before the Chinese could get their helicopters into the air.

I heard a faint sound. At first I thought it was the wind, but it gradually became louder. I hunkered down. Someone was calling my name. Finally I could see someone moving in the blowing snow. It was Wil.

I embraced him. "God, am I glad to see you. How did you find me?"

"I watched the direction the chopper flew in," he said, "and just kept walking until I saw the camp. I've been out here all night. If I hadn't had my camp stove with me, I would have frozen to death. I was trying to figure out how to get you out of there. But the blizzard solved that problem. Come on, we have to try again to get to the temples."

I hesitated.

"What's wrong?" Wil asked.

"Yin's in there," I replied. "He's hurt."

Wil thought for a moment as we looked back toward the compound. "They will be organizing a search party," he said. "We can't go back. We'll have to try to help him later. If we don't get out of here and find the temples before the colonel does, everything could be lost."

"What happened to Tashi?" I asked.

"We were separated when the avalanche started," Wil replied, "but I saw him later going on up the mountain alone."

We walked for more than two hours, and strangely, once we got out of the area around the Chinese encampment, the wind began to die down, although it was still snowing heavily. During our trek, I told Wil about everything that Yin had said in the tent, and what had happened with the colonel.

Finally we reached the area on the mountain where the avalanche had occurred. We hiked well past it and to the west, farther up the slope.

Without talking any more, Wil led the way upward for another two hours. Finally he stopped and sat down to rest behind a huge bank of snow.

We looked at each other for a long moment, both of us breathing hard. Wil smiled and asked, "Do you now understand what Yin was telling you?"

I was silent. Even though I had seen it all play out with the colonel, it still seemed hard to believe.

"I was engaging in negative prayer," I said finally. "That's how the colonel was able to follow me."

"We can go no farther until we both can avoid this," Wil said. "Our energy must stay consistently high before we can progress through the rest of the Fourth Extension. We must be very careful not to visualize the evilness of those who are in fear. We have to look at them realistically and take precautions, but if we dwell on their behavior or hold images that they are about to harm us, it sends energy to their paranoia and can actually give them the idea to do whatever it is that we expect. That's why it is so important not to let our minds visualize the bad things that could possibly happen to us. It is a prayer that acts to create that very event."

I shook my head, knowing I was still resisting this idea. If it was true, it seemed to put a high burden on each of us to watch every thought. I voiced my concern to Wil.

He almost laughed. "Of course we must monitor every thought. We have to do that in order not to miss an important intuition anyway. Besides, all that is necessary is to go back to a conscious alertness and always to visualize everyone's awareness being increased. The legends are very clear. To keep our prayer-energy extended most powerfully, we must never allow ourselves to use it negatively. We can go no farther until we can avoid this problem completely."

"How many of the legends were described to you?" I asked.

In answering my question, Wil began to talk about his experiences during this adventure in greater detail than he'd been able to before.

"When I came to your house," he began, "I was bewildered as to why my energy had fallen from where it was when we were exploring the Tenth Insight. Then I began to have thoughts of Tibet and found myself at the monastery of Lama Rigden, where I met Yin and heard of the dreams. I didn't understand it all, but I had similar dreams myself. I knew that you were involved ᵢmehow and had something to do here. That's when I began to study the legends in detail and to learn the prayer extensions. I was all set to meet you in Kathmandu, but I caught the Chinese following me, so I asked Yin to go instead. I had to trust that we would eventually find each other."

Wil paused a moment and dug out a white undershirt and began to put a new dressing on his knee. I looked out at the infinite expanse of white mountains behind us. The clouds parted for an instant and the morning sun created a rippling effect of light ridge tops and darker, shadowed valleys. The sight filled me with awe, and in a strange way I began to feel at home here, as though some part of me finally understood this land.

When I looked back at Wil, he was staring at me.

"Perhaps," Wil said, "we should go over all that the legends say about the prayer-field. We must understand how all this connects together."

I nodded.

"It all begins," he went on, "with the realization that our prayer-energy is real, that it flows out from us and affects the world.

"Once we have that realization, we can grasp that this field, this effect we have on the world, can be expanded, but we have to begin with the First Extension. We have to first improve the quality of energy we take in physically. Heavy and processed foods build up acid solids in our molecular structures, lowering our vibration and eventually causing disease. Alive foods have an alkaline effect and enhance our vibration.

"The purer we vibrate, the easier it is to then connect with the more subtle energies available within us. The legends say we will learn to consistently breathe in this higher level of energy using our increased perception of beauty as a measure. The higher our level of energy, the more beauty we see. We can learn to visualize this higher level of energy flowing out from us into the world, likewise using the emotional state of love as a measure that this is occurring.

"Thus we are connected within like we learned in Peru. Only now we've learned that by visualizing that energy is a field that goes out ahead of us wherever we go, we can stay consistently stronger.

"The Second Extension begins when we set this extended prayer-field to enhance the synchronistic flow of our lives. We do this by staying in a state of conscious alertness and expectation for the next intuition or coincidence that moves our lives further along. This expectation sends our energy out even farther and makes it stronger, because we are now aligning our intentions with the intended process of growth and evolution structured into the universe itself.

"The Third Extension involves another expectation: that our prayer-field go out and boost the level of energy in others, lifting them into their own connection with the divine within and into their own higher-self intuition. This, of course, increases the likelihood of them giving us intuitive information that can further enhance our own level of synchronicity. It is the interpersonal ethic we learned in Peru, only now we know how to use the prayer-field to make it stronger.

"The Fourth Extension begins when we learn the importance of anchoring and maintaining the outflow of our energy, in spite of fearful or angry situations. We do this by always maintaining a particular posture of detachment toward events as they occur, even as we expect the process itself to carry on. We must always seek a positive meaning, and always, always expect the process to save us, no matter what is happening. Such a mental posture helps us to stay focused on the flow and keeps us from dwelling on negative images of what might occur if we fail.

"In general, if we find a negative image coming to mind, we must consider whether it is an intuitive warning, and, if so, we need to take appropriate actions, but we must always return to the expectation that a higher synchronicity will guide us past this problem. This anchors our field, our outflow of energy, with a powerful expectation that has always been called faith.

"In sum, the first part of the Fourth Extension is about keeping our energy strong at all times. Once we master that, we can move forward and extend our energy even farther.

"The next step in the Fourth Extension begins when we fully expect that the human world can move toward the ideal expressed in the Tenth Insight and modeled by Shambhala. Moving your energy out farther and stronger in this way takes true belief. That's why understanding Shambhala is so important. Knowing that Shambhala has done it extends our expectation that the rest of human culture can do it too. We can readily see how humans everywhere can master our technology and use it in the service of our spiritual development, and then begin to focus on the life process itself, on the real reason we are here on this planet: to create a culture on Earth that is conscious of our role in spiritual evolution and to teach that understanding to our children."

He stopped and looked at me for a moment.

"Now comes the most difficult part," he said. "To expand even farther, we must do more than just remain positive in general, and avoid images of negative events occurring. We must also keep all negative thoughts out of our heads concerning other people. As you have just seen, if our fear ever turns to anger and we lapse into thinking the worst of others, a negative prayer goes out that tends to create in them exactly the behavior we expect. That's why teachers who expect great things from their students usually get it, and when they expect the negative, they get that too.

"Most people believe it is a bad thing to say something negative about others, but that it's okay to think it. We now know it's not okay; thoughts matter."

As Wil said this, I thought about the recent spate of school shootings by students in the United States, and mentioned what I was thinking to Wil.

"Kids everywhere," he said, "are more powerful than ever, and the typical cliques and put-downs that have always occurred in schools can't be ignored by teachers any longer. When certain kids are looked down on and made fun of and scapegoated, they are affected by this negative prayer more than ever before. They now sometimes strike back explosively.

"And this is not just happening with kids; it's happening throughout human culture. Only by understanding the effect of prayer-fields can we grasp what is happening. We all are gradually growing more powerful, and if we don't become completely mindful of our expectations, we can inadvertently cause great harm to others."

Wil stopped talking and raised his eyebrow. "That brings us up to where we are now, I believe."

I nodded, realizing how much I had missed him.

"Where do the legends say we go from here?" I asked.

"To the subject I have been most interested in," he replied. "The legends say that we can't expand our fields farther until we fully acknowledge the dakini."

I quickly told him about my many experiences with the strange figures and lighted areas since coming to Tibet.

"You had those experiences before Tibet," Wil said.

He was right. There were times when we were looking for the Tenth Insight that I seemed to be helped by strange wisps of light.

"That's right," I said, "when we were together in the Appalachians."

"In Peru too," he added.

I tried to remember but nothing came to mind.

"You told me about the time you faced a crossroads and didn't know which way to go," he said. "And one road appeared more lit up, more luminous, and you chose that direction."

"Yes," I said, remembering the occurrence clearly. "You think that was a dakini?"

Wil was standing on his feet, putting on his pack.

"Yes," he said. "They are the luminosities we see that guide our way."

I was dumbfounded. That meant that whenever we experience a luminous object or a pathway that seems brighter and more attractive or a book that jumps out at us and draws our attention to it—it is the work of these beings.

"What else do the legends say about the dakini?" I asked.

"That they are the same for every culture, every religion, no matter what we call them."

I gave him a questioning look.

"We could call them angels," Wil continued, "but no matter whether they are called dakini or angels, they are the same beings . . . and they do their work in the same way."

I had another question to ask, but Wil was hurrying up the slope, avoiding the areas of heavy show. I followed, dozens of questions coming to my mind. I didn't want to let the conversation go.

At one point Wil glanced back at me. "The legends say these beings have aided humans since the beginning of time, and they are spoken of in the mystical literature of every religion. According to the legends, each of us will begin to perceive them more readily. If we really acknowledge them, the dakini will make themselves more known."

The way he was stressing the word "acknowledge" made me think it had a special meaning.

"But how do we do this?" I asked, climbing over a rock that was jutting out into the path.

Wil stopped above me and let me catch up, then said, "According to the legends, we have to really acknowledge that they are there. That is very difficult for our modern minds to do. It is one thing to think the dakini or angels are a fascinating subject matter. It is another thing altogether to expect them to be perceivable in our lives."

"What are you saying we should do?"

"Watch alertly for every shade of luminosity."

"So if we keep our energy high and acknowledge them," I said, "then we can begin to see more of the luminosities?"

"That's right," he said. "The hard part is training ourselves to look for the subtle changes in the light around us. But if we do, we can detect it more."

I thought about what he was saying and I understood, as far as it went, but I still had a question. "What about the cases," I asked, "of dakini or angels intervening directly in our lives when we aren't expecting them or acknowledging them? This has happened to me."

I went on to tell Wil about the tall figure that had been there when Yin pushed me out of the Jeep north of Ali, and had showed up again when the campfire appeared at the ruined monastery, before I entered Shambhala.

Wil was nodding. "It appears your guardian angel has shown himself. The legends say each of us has one."

I paused, looking at him.

"Then the myths are true," I said finally. "We each have a guardian angel."

My mind was going a hundred miles an hour. The reality of these beings had never been so clear.

"But what makes them help us at certain times," I asked, "and not others?"

Will raised his eyebrow. "That," he said, "is the secret we are here to discover."

We were reaching the summit of the mountain. Behind us the sun was beginning to break through the thick overcast and it felt as if the temperature was warning.

"I was told," Wil said, stopping just short of the mountain's top, "that the temples are on the other side of this ridge."

He stopped and looked at me. "This may be the hardest part."

His words sounded ominous to me.

"Why?" I asked. "What do you mean?"

"We have to put all the extensions together and keep our energy as strong as possible. The legends say that only if we are able to keep our energy high enough will we be able to see the temples."

At exactly this moment, we heard helicopters somewhere in the distance.

"And don't forget what you just learned," Wil said. "If you start to think about the evil in the Chinese military, if you feel anger or disgust, you must shift your attention immediately to the soul in each soldier that can emerge. Visualize your energy flowing out from you and entering their fields, lifting them into a connection with the light inside, so that they can discover their higher intuitions. To do otherwise is to send a prayer out that gives them more energy to be evil."

I nodded and looked down. I was determined to maintain this positive field.

"Now, go beyond that to acknowledge the dakini and expect the luminosities."

I looked out at the summit just ahead, and Wil nodded and

led the way forward. When we reached the crest, we could see nothing on the other side except a series of snow-covered peaks and valleys. We surveyed the scene carefully.

"Over there," Wil yelled, pointing to our left.

I strained to see. Something at the edge of the crest seemed to be shimmering slightly. When I tried to focus on it directly, all I saw was that the area seemed luminous. But when I looked at it through the corner of my eye, I could tell that the space itself was shimmering.

"Let's go," Wil said. He pulled my arm as we made our way across the deep snow and up to the spot we'd seen. As we walked closer, the area seemed to grow brighter still. Beyond it was a series of huge, rocky spires that looked from a distance to be lined up side by side. Upon closer inspection, however, we found that one was set back from the others, leaving a narrow passage that bent around farther to the left and down the slope of the mountain. When we reached the passage, we discovered that there were actually stone steps, hewn into the rocks, that led that way downward. The steps also appeared luminous and were clear of snow.

"The dakini are showing us where to go," Wil said, still pulling me along.

We ducked through the opening and followed the descending pathway. On both sides, a sheer rock face rose upward twenty or thirty feet and blocked out most of the light. For more than an hour we walked down the steps, steadily descending until at last the cliffs widened above our heads.

Several yards farther the ground leveled off and the steps ended. We found ourselves looking out on a flat precipice that wrapped around the rock face to the left.

"Over there," Wil said, pointing.

Two hundred yards ahead of us appeared to be an old monastery, totally in ruin, as if it were thousands of years old. As we walked toward it, the temperature warmed even more and a misty ground fog rose from the rocks. In front of the monastery, the precipice widened into a wide shelf that cut into the side of the mountain. When we reached the ruins, we carefully made our way through the collapsed walls and large stones until we emerged on the other side.

There, we were stopped in our tracks. The rocky surface we were walking on had turned to a floor of smooth flat stones, light amber in color, that were evenly placed onto the ground beneath our feet. I glanced at Wil, who was looking straight ahead. In front of us was an intact temple, standing fifty feet high and twice that wide. It was rusty brown with streaks of gray along the joints of the fitted stone walls. On the front were two mammoth doors, fifteen or twenty feet high.

Something moved in the misty fog near the temple. I looked at Wil and he nodded, motioning me to follow him. We walked to within twenty yards of the structure.

"What was that movement?" I asked Wil.

He gestured with his head toward the area in front of us. Less than ten feet away was a form of some kind.

I strained to focus and finally was able to detect the barest outline of a human figure.

"It must be one of the adepts who inhabit the temples," Wil said. "The person is vibrating higher than us. That's why we can only see a hazy shape."

As we watched, the shape moved toward the door of the temple and disappeared. Wil led the way up to the door. It appeared to be made of some kind of stone, yet when Wil pulled it by the carved stone knob, it glided open as though it weighed nothing.

Inside was a large circular room, sloping downward in a series of terraced steps toward a center, stagelike area. As I surveyed the structure, I caught sight of another figure halfway to the stage, only this person was clear to our perception. He turned so we could see his face. It was Tashi. Wil was already moving toward him.

Before we reached Tashi, a spatial window appeared in the space just above the center of the room. The image slowly came into focus, captivating our attention, and growing so bright we could no longer see Tashi. It was a view of the Earth, seen from space.

The scene shifted in quick succession to a view of a city, somewhere in Europe, and then to a metropolitan area in the United States, and finally to one in Asia. In each case we could see people walking on busy streets, as well as some in offices or other work environments. As the scene again shifted through different cities in different areas of the planet, we could see that the individuals, as they worked and interacted, were slowly raising their energy levels.

We began to see and hear individuals involved in moving from one type of occupation to another, following their intuitions, and growing more inspired and creative as they did so, inventing new and faster technologies and more efficient services. At the same time we also began to see scenes of people who were still in fear, resisting the changes and trying to gain control.

Next we focused on a research facility, inside a conference room. A group of men and women was engaged in a heated exchange. As we watched and listened, the content of the conversation became clear. Most of the people were in favor of a new coalition between the larger communications and computer companies and an international group of intelligence services. The representatives of the intelligence services argued that the fight against terrorism necessitated having access to every telephone line, including Internet communications, and secret identification devices in all computers so that authorities could go in and monitor anyone's files.

But that wasn't all. They wanted more surveillance systems. Several of the people were even speculating that if the problem of computer viruses continued, the Internet might have to be taken over completely, along with all linked computers in commerce everywhere. Access could be controlled but a special ID number that would be required in order to do any electronically based business.

One hypothesized that new identification systems might have to be implemented for this use, such as iris or palm scans or perhaps even something based on brain wave patterns themselves.

Two other people, a man and a woman, started arguing vehemently against these measures. One mentioned the book of Revelation and the mark of the beast. As we continued to watch and listen, I realized I could see through the window of the conference room. A car was passing along a road outside the building. In the background I could see cactus and miles of desert.

I looked at Wil.

"This discussion is happening right now," he said, "in present time somewhere. It looks like the southwestern United States."

Directly behind the table where the group was gathered, I noticed something else. The space around them was becoming larger. No, it was becoming lighter.

"The dakini!" I said to Wil.

We continued to watch as the conversation began to change. The two people who were arguing against the extreme surveillance seemed to be gaining more attention from the group. The proponents seemed to be reconsidering.

Without warning, our attention was pulled away from the image in front of us by a sharp vibration that shook the floor and walls of the temple. We ran for another door at the end of the building, fighting to see though the dust. We could hear stones crumbling and falling outside. When we were thirty feet from the door, it opened and a figure we couldn't make out quickly moved through it.

"That must have been Tashi," Wil said as he rushed to the door and pulled it open.

As we ran through the opening, another booming crash filled the air behind us. The old ruin we had first seen was collapsing in an implosion of rocks and dust. Behind it somewhere we could hear the roar of helicopters.

"The colonel seems to be following us again," I said. "But I'm holding only positive images in my mind, so how is he doing that?"

Wil looked at me questioningly, and I remembered Colonel Chang's remark about how he now had the technology so that I could never get away. He had my brain scan.

I quickly told Wil what had happened, then said, "Maybe I should go in another direction, lead the soldiers out of the temples."

"No," Wil said. "You have to be here. You're going to be needed. We'll have to stay ahead of them until we find Tashi."

We followed a stone pathway past several other temples, and I found my eyes lingering on a doorway to our left.

Wil turned, noticing.

"Why were you looking at that door?" he asked.

"I don't know," I replied. "It caught my eye."

He gave me an incredulous look.

"Oh yeah, right," I said quickly. "Let's check it out."

We ran inside and I found another circular room, this one much larger, perhaps several hundred feet in diameter. Another spatial window was hovering over the center. As we entered, I saw Tashi to our right a few yards away, and nudged Wil.

"I see him," Wil said, leading the way in the near darkness to join the boy.

Tashi turned around and saw us, then smiled in relief, before focusing again on the scene visible through the window. This time we were seeing a room filled with the things of youth: pictures, balls, various games, piles of clothes. A bed was in disarray in the corner, and a carry-out pizza box littered one end of a table. At the other end of the table, a teenager of about fifteen worked on something, some kind of wired apparatus. He was dressed in shorts without a shirt, and his face seemed angry and determined.

As we continued to watch, the scene though the window shifted to another room, where another teenager, dressed in jeans and a sweatshirt, sat on a bed staring at a phone. He got up and paced across the room several times and then sat down again. I got the impression that he was struggling with a decision. Finally he picked up the phone and dialed a number.

At that point the window widened so that we could see both scenes. The boy with no shirt answered the phone. The youth in the sweatshirt seemed to be pleading, and the other boy grew ever more angry. Finally the shirtless boy slammed down the phone, sat down, and began working at the table again.

The other teenager got up and put on a coat and hurried out the door. In a few minutes the boy at the table heard a knock and got up and walked over to the door of his room and opened it. It was the youth he had been talking to on the phone. He tried to shut the door, but the boy pushed his way in, continuing to talk to him in pleading gestures, pointing at the apparatus on the table.

The other teenager pushed him back and pulled a gun from a drawer and pointed it at his visitor. This boy stepped back but continued to plead. The youth with the gun exploded with anger and pushed his victim hard against a wall, placing the barrel of the gun against his temple.

At this moment, in the area behind them both, we began to detect a change: The area was getting lighter.

I glanced at Tashi, who met my gaze for an instant and then focused again on the scene. We both knew we were again witnessing the dakini at work.

As we watched, the one boy continued to plead and the other held him firm against the wall. But gradually the boy with the gun began to relax. Finally he dropped the gun to his side and went over and sat on the edge of the bed. The other youth sat down in a chair facing him.

Now we could hear the details of their conversation, and it became clear that the boy who had the gun wanted to be accepted by others at his school, but had not been. Many of his peers were excelling at extracurricular activities, expanding their talents, and he didn't have the confidence to keep up. They had been kidding him, calling him a loser, and he felt as though he was a nobody, that he was fading away. The situation filled him with anger and a false sense of strength, which had led him to decide to fight back. The device he had been working on was a homemade bomb.

Just as before, we felt a jolt under our feet, and the whole building shook. We all ran for the door and had just made it out when half the temple collapsed behind us.

Tashi motioned for us to follow him, and we ran several hundred yards and stopped beside a wall.

"Could you see the people in the temple," he asked, "the ones who were sending prayer-energy to the boys?"

We both confessed we could not.

"There were hundreds in there," he said, "working on the problem of youth anger."

"What were they doing exactly?" I asked.

Tashi stepped toward me. "They were extending their prayer-energy, visualizing the boys in that scene lifted into a higher vibration so they could move past their fear and anger and find their higher intuitions to resolve the situation. Their energy helped the one youth find the best, most persuasive ideas. In the case of the other youth, the extra prayer-energy lifted him into an identity above and beyond the social self his peers rejected. He no longer felt that in order to be someone, he needed their approval. It eased his anger."

"And that's what they were doing in the other temple as well?" I asked. "Helping to counter those who want to control everything?"

Wil looked at me. "The people in the temple were sending out a prayer-field aimed at helping to raise the energy level of everyone involved, which had the effect of easing the fear of those who were pressing for ever more surveillance, and helping those who were resisting to find the courage to speak, even within those kinds of organizations."

Tashi was nodding. "We are supposed to be seeing this. These are some of the key situations that must be won if spiritual evolution is to continue, if we are to get past this critical point in history."

"What about the dakini?" I asked. "What were they doing?"

"They were helping lift the energy level as well," Tashi replied.

"Yeah," I pressed, "but we still don't know what makes them go there and take action. Those in the temples were doing something else we don't know yet."

At that moment another loud noise filled the air as the other half of the temple behind us crashed to the ground.

Tashi jumped involuntarily, then hurried down the pathway.

"Come on," he said. "We have to find my grandmother."

11

THE SECRET OF
SHAMBHALA

For hours, we wandered through the temples, looking for Tashi's grandmother, hurrying to stay ahead of the Chinese military,
and observing the work those in the temples were doing. In each
temple, we found people viewing a situation in the outer cultures
that seemed critical.

One temple was focused on other problems related to youth
alienation—the proliferation of violent experiences induced by
movies and killer video games, which created the delusion that
violent acts could be performed in anger and then erased somehow without being final, a false reality that was at the heart of
the school shootings.

In these instances, we watched as the creators of these games
were each sent energy that had the effect, as before, of lifting
them into a higher intuitive perspective with which they could
rethink the effects of their creations on children. At the same
time, key parents were likewise being lifted into higher energy
states, where they could investigate their hunches about what
their children were doing and find more time to model a different
reality.

One temple focused on the current debate within the field of medicine over alternative, preventive approaches—approaches that were being proved to be beneficial in the elimination of disease and in the increase of longevity. The gatekeepers of medicine—the medical organizations of various countries, the heads of popular research clinics, the government institutes of health who dispensed large financial grants, the pharmaceutical companies—all operated out of an eighteenth-century paradigm which fought the symptoms of disease without much thought about prevention.

Their targets were various microbes, faulty genes, and runaway tumor cells—and most thought such problems were the inevitable results of aging. Under this point of view, the huge majority of grant money was going to the large research facilities looking for magic bullets: pharmaceuticals that could be patented and sold to kill the microbes, destroy the malignant cells, or somehow reprogram the genes. Almost no money was going into research to discover ways to boost the immune system and prevent such diseases.

In one scene we watched, a conference meeting involving representatives for many medical fields, some scientists were arguing that the entire field of medicine had to change its point of view if we were ever going to solve the riddle of human disease, including the arterial lesions of heart disease, the tumors of cancer, and the degenerative illnesses such as arthritis and lupus and MS.

These scientists were arguing—as Hanh had earlier—that the true cause of disease of every type was the polluting of the body's basic environment by the foods we were eating and other toxins, shifting the body from the healthy, vibrant, alkaline state of youth, to a dull, low-energy acid state, which created a climate in which microbes flourish and begin to systematically decompose the body. Every ailment, they argued, is the result of this slow decomposition of our cells by microbes, but they don't attack us without cause. It is the foods we consume that set us up for these problems.

Others in the room had trouble accepting these findings. Something had to be wrong, they thought. How could human illness be that simple? They were involved with health industries which saw consumers spending billions of dollars on complex drugs and expensive surgeries. The health officials in the room had to believe all this was necessary. Some were dedicated to the proposal, close to being accepted in many countries, that chips should be placed in every individual to store health and drug information, a control and identification ability that the intelligence services also wanted. They were committed to this program. Their positions of power depended on it. Their very livelihoods were at stake.

Besides, they personally loved the foods they ate. How could they recommend that people change their diets in ways they couldn't imagine doing themselves? No, they couldn't accept this.

Still, the physicians with the new research continued to plead their case, knowing the climate was right to change the paradigm. Look at how the rain forests were being cleared and destroyed to raise beef for the Western countries, they argued, a problem ever more people were becoming aware of.

Also helpful was the fact that baby boomers in all countries were beginning to reach ages when diseases strike, and they had already seen the medical establishment fail their parents. They were looking for new alternatives.

Slowly we saw the conflict begin to moderate in the conference we were watching. Those arguing for the alternative approaches were being listened to.

In another temple, we witnessed the same kind of debate in

the profession of law. A group of attorneys was urging the profession to begin to police itself. For years, reputable attorneys had stood by and watched many of their colleagues engage in the practice of manufacturing lawsuits, coaching witnesses to shade the truth, inventing imaginary defenses, and hypnotizing juries. Now there was a movement to raise the standards. Certain attorneys were arguing that they must move to a higher vision of what they do, that they must understand the true role of lawyers: to reduce conflict, not promote it.

Similarly, several of the temples we saw were looking at the situation of political corruption in various countries. We saw scenes of elected officials in Washington, D.C., debating behind closed doors as to whether to support campaign finance reform. At issue, most especially, was the ability of political parties to receive unlimited amounts of contributions from special interests and spend it on general TV spots which distorted the truth in any manner they wished. This dependence on large corporations for these funds obviously obligated the politicians of the party to certain favors. And everyone knew it.

These politicians resisted the arguments of reformers that democracy could never reach its ideal until it was based not on distorted TV ads, but on public debates—where the citizens could more readily judge demeanor, facial expression, and truthfulness, and thus use their intuition to choose the best candidate.

As we continued to move through the temples, it became clear that all of them were similarly focused on some particular area of human life. We saw many fearful world leaders, including those in the Chinese government, being helped to join the global community and to implement economic and social reforms.

And in every case, the area behind the people involved would lighten and then those most in fear, who were acting to control or manipulate to ensure personal gain or power, would gradually begin to lessen the intractability of their positions.

As we continued to run through the maze of temples searching for Tashi's grandmother, the same questions kept coming to me. What, exactly, was happening here? What was the relationship between the dakini or the angels and the prayer extensions being performed? What did those in the temples know that we didn't?

At one point we stood facing literally miles of temples as far as we could see. The paths were going in every direction. In the background we could still hear the helicopters. As we stood there, another large temple, five hundred feet behind us, came crashing to the ground.

"What's happening to the people inside those temples?" I asked Tashi.

He stared at the plume of dust rising from the rubble. "Don't worry, they're all right. They can move into another location without being seen. The problem is that their role of sending energy is being disrupted."

He looked at both of us. "If they aren't able to help with these situations, who's going to?"

Wil walked over to Tashi. "We have to decide where to go. We don't have much time."

"My grandmother is out there somewhere," he said. "My father told me she is at one of the central temples."

I looked out at the maze of stoned structures. "There is no physical center, not that I can see."

"That's not what my father meant," Tashi said. "He meant that Grandmother is at a temple that is focused on the central, end-point issues of human evolution." Tashi was surveying the temples in the distance as he spoke.

"You can see the people here better than us," I said to him. "Could you talk to them and ask them where to go?"

"I tried to talk to them," he replied, "but my energy isn't strong enough. Possibly if I was able to stay here for a little while."

Tashi had no sooner finished his sentence than another temple crashed to the ground, this time much closer.

"We have to stay ahead of the soldiers' energy," Wil said.

"Wait a minute," Tashi said. "I think I see something."

He was looking out toward the maze of temples. I surveyed the scene as well, seeing nothing different. When I glanced at Wil, he shrugged.

"Where?" I asked Tashi.

He was already walking down a pathway to the right, motioning for us to follow.

After hurriedly walking for twenty minutes we stopped in front of a temple whose architecture was much the same as all the others, except that it was larger and its dark brown rock carried a slightly bluer hue.

Tashi stood motionless, looking directly at the massive stone door.

"What is it, Tashi?" Wil asked.

Far behind us we heard a crash as yet another temple collapsed.

Tashi looked over at me. "The temple in your dream, the one where you said we found someone? Wasn't it blue?"

I looked at the temple again. "Yeah," I said. "It was."

Wil walked toward the door and looked back at us.

Tashi nodded, and Wil swung the huge rock slab back on its hinges.

The temple was filled with people. As before, I could only see the slight outlines of many bodies. They all seemed to be moving, gathering around us, and I felt awash in a distinct feeling of joy. They were moving in a way that gave me the impression that they were turning toward the center of the temple. Turning that way myself, I saw a spatial window open. We began to see various scenes in the Middle East, followed by images from the Vatican, then Asia, all seemingly indicating a growing dialogue between the major institutional religions.

We watched scenes that showed how an increased tolerance was developing. In Christianity, in both the Catholic and Protestant traditions, it was becoming understood that the true conversion experience within Christianity and the true devotional and enlightenment experiences of the Eastern religions, Judaism, and Islam—the experience itself—were exactly the same. It was just that each religion emphasized different aspects of this mystical interaction with God.

The Eastern religions emphasized the effects on consciousness itself, the experience of lightness, a sense of oneness with the universe, the release of the ego's desires, and a certain detachment. Islam emphasized the feeling of unity that came with sharing this experience with others and the power inherent in group action. Judaism emphasized the importance of a tradition based on this connection, of the experience of feeling chosen, and that each person alive is responsible for pushing forward the evolution of human spirituality.

Christianity was emphasizing the idea that the spirit manifests in human beings not just as an increased awareness of being part of God but also as a higher self—as though we become an expanded version of who we are, more complete, capable, with an inner guidance and wisdom leading us to act, as if the human personality of God, the Christ, was now looking through our eyes.

In the scene before us, we could see the effects of this new tolerance and unity. More and more the focus was being placed on the experience of connection itself, not on differences of emphasis. There seemed to be a growing willingness to resolve ethnic and religious conflicts, a greater communication between religious leaders, and a new understanding of how powerful prayer could be, if all extended their fields in religious unity.

As I watched, I understood fully what Lama Rigden and Ani had both said about the unification of religion, that this would be a sign that the secrets of Shambhala were becoming known.

At that point the scene through the window in front of us changed. We could see a group of people talking and joyously celebrating the birth of a baby. Everyone was laughing and passing the infant from one person to another. The people looked to be different from each other, representing various nationalities. As I watched, I got the distinct impression that they represented different religious backgrounds as well. As I looked closely, I could see the parents of the baby. They looked familiar. I knew it was not them, but the parents' facial features were very similar to Pema's and her husband's.

I strained to see, getting the feeling that we were now being shown something of immense importance. What was it?

The scene changed again, and we were now looking at a tropical region which looked like Southeast Asia or perhaps China. As before, the scene shifted into a house where a number of people, diverse in appearance, were taking turns holding a newborn and toasting the parents.

"Don't you see what we're being shown?" Tashi said. "That's

where the missing conceptions were going. They were moving to different families, all over the world. It must have been a channeling process. Somehow the children were gaining the higher genetic energy of Shambhala before moving on."

Wil was looking down, thinking, then he stared back at us.

"That's the shift," he said. "That's what the legends have been talking about. Shambhala's not moving to one place; its energy is moving to many different locations all over the globe."

"What?" I asked.

Tashi looked over at me. "You know the legend that says the warriors of Shambhala will stream out of the east and defeat the powers of darkness, and create an ideal society. This isn't happening with horses and swords. It's happening with the effect of our extended fields, as the knowledge of Shambhala moves into the world. If all those from every religion who believe strongly in a connection with the divine avoid negative prayer and work together, we can all use the prayer extensions to take over the role of Shambhala."

"But we don't know everything they're doing," I said. "We don't know the rest of the secret!"

Just as I said that, the scene through the spatial window changed again. Now we could see a great expanse of snow-covered mountains and a group of Chinese military helicopters heading toward us. We saw more temples begin to crumble to the ground as they approached, taking on the appearance of ancient ruins and then fading away altogether to dust. The scene switched to the outside of the very building where we were, and then inside.

We saw ourselves standing in the building, and all around us were not hazy outlines of people but clear pictures of them. Many were adorned in the formal attire of Tibetan monks, but many others were dressed differently. Some appeared in the clothing of the Eastern religions, others wore the traditional attire of Hasidic Jews, and still others wore the robes and carried the crucifixes of Christianity. Just as many were dressed as Islamic mullahs.

Interestingly one of them reminded me of a person living near my house in the valley, and my eyes lingered on her. I slipped into a daydream about home. In my mind's eye, I could see everything very clearly: the mountains viewed from my front window, and then the same view from the spring. I thought of the taste of the water there. I pictured myself leaning over and drinking.

Again we could hear the roar of helicopters, very near to us, and the sound of one of the other temples crashing to the ground.

Tashi had turned away and walked over to our right. In the scene through the spatial window, we could see what he was doing. Tashi was facing one of the Tibetan monks.

"Who is that?" I asked Wil.

"It must be his grandmother," Wil replied.

They were clearly speaking to each other, but I couldn't quite understand the words. Finally the two embraced and Tashi rushed over to us.

I was still watching Tashi through the window, but when he reached me, the scene disappeared. The window was still there, but the images within it were fuzzy, like a television set tuned to a nonexistent channel.

Tashi was glowing. "Don't you see?" he said. "This is the temple where they have been watching you and Wil the whole time you were trying to reach Shambhala. These people are the ones who have been using their prayer-field to help you. Without them none of us would be here."

I looked around and realized I could no longer see the outlines of anyone around us.

"Where did they go?" I yelled.

"They had to leave," Tashi replied, now staring up at the empty window hovering in the center of the room. "It's up to us now."

At that moment a huge shock reverberated through the temple and several stones thudded to the ground outside.

"It's the soldiers," Tashi yelled. "They're here." He was looking toward the sound of the helicopters outside.

Without warning, the spatial window cleared and we could see the Chinese getting out of their helicopters right outside. Colonel Chang walked to the front, giving directions to his troops. We could see his face clearly.

"We've got to uplift him with our fields," Wil said.

Tashi nodded in agreement and quickly led us through the extensions. We visualized our energy fields overflowing out of us and into the fields of the Chinese soldiers, especially Chang, lifting them to a new awareness of their higher intuitions.

As I watched his face, he seemed to pause and look up, as if sensing the higher energy.

I looked closely for any expression of his higher self, and noticed what seemed to be a slight shift in his eyes, maybe even a half-smile. He seemed to be looking around at his soldiers.

"Focus on his face," I said. "On his face."

As we did this, he seemed to pause again. One of the soldiers, apparently next in command, walked up to him and began asking him questions. For a moment or two, Chang ignored the junior officer. But slowly the subordinate gained his attention, pointing at the temple we were in. Chang seemed to regain his focus, and an angry expression returned to his face. He motioned for all the soldiers to follow him as he headed toward us.

"It's not working," I said.

Wil looked at me. "The dakini aren't here."

"We have to leave," Tashi shouted.

"How?" Wil asked.

Tashi turned to face us. "We have to go through the window. My grandmother told me that we could leave through the window to the outer cultures. But only if we had help from that location to raise the energy on the other side."

"What did she mean, help?" I asked. "Who would help?"

Tashi shook his head. "I don't know."

"Well, we've got to try," Wil shouted. "Now!"

Tashi appeared confused.

"How did you go through the windows back in the outer rings?" I asked.

"We had the amplifiers back there," he replied. "I'm not sure I can do it without them."

I touched Tashi's shoulder. "Ani said that everyone in the rings was on the verge of being able to manifest without the technology. Think. How did you do it?"

Tashi was still struggling. "I don't know, really. It was sort of automatic." He paused. "I guess we just expected it to occur and it would happen instantly."

"Do that, Tashi," Wil said, nodding toward the window. "Do it now."

I could tell Tashi was concentrating totally, and then he looked at me. "I have to know where I want to go so I can visualize it. Where are we supposed to go?"

"Wait a minute," I said. "What about the dream you had? Weren't you seeing water?"

Tashi thought for a moment, then said, "It was at a place overlooking a source of water. A well maybe, or a . . ."

"A spring?" I shouted. "A spring with a walled-off pool made of stone?"

He stared at me for a moment. "I think so."

I looked at Wil. "I know where it is. It's a spring on the north ridge of the valley where I live. That's where we have to go."

At that moment the temple shook violently again. Images of the temple collapsing or explosions blowing us away filled my mind and I shook them off, imaging instead that we would escape. I began to feel like my father, caught in a battle I had not asked for but, because of the stakes, was unable to avoid. Only it was a battle of the mind.

"Focus," I yelled. "What do we do?"

"We first have to visualize where we are going," Tashi replied. "Describe it to us."

Hastily I told them every detail: the mountain path, the trees, the way the water flowed, the color of the foliage this time of year. Then we all tried to help as Tashi concentrated on the image. As we watched, the window shifted to that very site. We could see the spring clearly.

"That's it!" I shouted.

Wil turned to Tashi. "Now what? Your grandmother said we would need help."

Through the window we caught sight of a person in the background, and we all focused on the fuzzy image. I struggled to make out who it was, noticing that the individual looked young, in fact about Tashi's age.

Finally the picture cleared, and I recognized who it was.

"It's Natalie, my neighbor's daughter," I shouted, remembering my first intuition of her. It was of this scene.

Tashi was smiling broadly. "That's my sister!"

At that moment another huge piece of the temple crashed to the ground outside.

"She's helping us," Wil yelled, pushing us all toward the window. "Let's go!"

With a swooshing sound, Tashi ducked through, followed by

Wil. Just as I approached the window, the back wall of the temple fell in, and there, on the other side, stood Colonel Chang.

I turned and glanced at him, then moved into the window.

His face was still determined as he grabbed a shortwave radio off his belt.

"I know where you're going!" he shouted as the rest of the temple began to fall in. "I know!"

When I stepped through the window, my foot landed on familiar soil, and I felt the warm air on my face. I was back at home.

As I looked around, I noticed that Tashi and Natalie were standing together, looking into each other's eyes, talking rapidly. Their faces were elated, as though they had just discovered something. Wil stood by their side.

Behind them was Natalie's father, Bill, and several other neighbors from around the community, including Father Brannigan and Sri Devo, and Julie Carmichael, a Protestant minister. All of them looked slightly confused.

Bill walked over to me.

"I don't know where you came from but thank God you're here."

I pointed toward the clerics. "What is everyone doing here?"

"Natalie asked them to come. She's been talking about legends and showing us how to create prayer-fields, all sorts of things. Apparently these ideas have just been coming to her. She said she could see what was happening to you, and we've been seeing someone watching your house."

I looked up the hill and was about to say something when Bill interrupted. "Natalie also said something strange. She said she had a brother. Who is that kid she's talking to?"

"I'll explain later," I said. "Who has been watching my house:

Bill didn't answer. He was watching as Wil and the others were walking up to us.

At that moment we heard vehicles approaching on the hill above us. A blue van pulled up to my house. Two men got out, saw us, and walked out to an overhang a hundred feet above us.

"They're Chinese Intelligence," Wil said. "Chang must have alerted them. We have to create a field."

I was expecting the clerics to ask what that was, but instead they nodded in agreement. Natalie began to lead us through the extensions, Tashi at her side.

"Begin with the energy of the creator," she said. "Let it come into your body and fill you up. Let it flow out the top of your head and through your eyes. Let it flow out into the world in a constant prayer-field until you see only beauty and feel only love. In a heightened alertness, expect this field to move out and boost the spiritual fields of the men above us, raising them into their intuitions."

Up on the hill, the men stared ominously and started down the path toward us.

Tashi looked over at Natalie and nodded.

"Now," Natalie began, "we can empower the angels."

I glanced at Wil. "What?"

"First," Natalie continued, "we must make sure our fields are fully set to enter the fields of the men up there. See it happening. They aren't enemies, they're people, souls in fear. And then we must acknowledge the angels fully, and very deliberately visualize them coming to the men.

"Then with all your expectations, visualize them amplifying our prayer-fields. Empower the angels fully to energize the higher selves of those men beyond what we can do alone, uplifting the men into an awareness that is incapable of evil."

I was staring at the two men on the hill, searching for the lighter area that would indicate the presence of the dakini, struggling to focus but seeing nothing.

"It's not working," I said to Wil.

"Look!" he shouted. "Up there to the right."

As I stared, I began to detect a light approaching, then noticed that the light was surrounding a person who was walking toward the two men. The man surrounded by the light had on the uniform of a deputy sheriff.

"Who is that officer?" I asked Bill. "He looks familiar."

"Wait," Wil said. "It's not a person."

I looked again and watched as the deputy began to talk with the two men. The light surrounded them and they finally walked back toward their vehicle. Although the deputy remained where he was, the light extended out to them and surrounded the van. They quickly left.

"The extension worked," Wil said.

I wasn't really listening. My eyes were focused on the deputy, who had turned toward us. He was tall and had black hair. Where had I seen him before?

It came to me as he turned and walked away. This was the same man I had seen at the pool in Kathmandu, the one who had first told me about the prayer research, the one I had glimpsed on several other occasions, the one Wil had called my guardian angel.

"They've always posed as humans when necessary," Tashi said, walking up to me with Natalie.

"We have just completed the last extension," Tashi added. "We finally know the secret of Shambhala. We can now begin to perform as those in Shambhala have done. They have looked out on the world and found key situations that were occurring and then interceded with not only the strength of their own prayer-field but the strength of the angelic realms as well. This is the role of the angels, to amplify."

"I don't understand," I said. "Why didn't it work when we tried to stop Chang just before we came through the window?"

"I didn't know the last step," Tashi said. "I didn't realize what those in the temples were doing until I could talk to Natalie. We had been uplifting Chang, which was necessary, but we didn't know to empower the angelic forces to come in on our energy and intervene. We have to begin with acknowledging the angels, but then, at this level of energy, we have to empower them to act. We must do this very intentionally. We must ask them to come."

Tashi stopped and looked out thoughtfully toward the horizon, a smile breaking out on his face.

"What is it, Tashi?" I asked.

"It's Ani and the rest of Shambhala," he said. "They're linking with us. I can feel them."

He asked for everyone's attention. "There's one more thing we can do. We can empower the angels in a general way to protect this valley."

We followed along as Natalie led us through the process of setting a special field to flow out to the tops of the wooded ridges in all directions around the valley, and to empower the angels to protect us.

"Visualize an angel being stationed on each ridge," she said. "Shambhala was always protected. We can be protected too."

We all continued to focus on the mountains for several more minutes, then the two youths began another intense conversation between themselves, as we listened.

They were talking about the other kids who had come through Shambhala, and the need for them to wake up, wherever they are. They told us that the kids coming in right now are more powerful than ever before. They're bigger, stronger, more

intelligent in a whole new way. More are involved in extracurricular activities than ever before. They sing, dance, play a greater
variety of sports, make music, write. More of them are developing their talents at an earlier age than was ever seen in previous
generations.

"There's only one problem. The force of their expectation is
much greater, but they haven't learned to fully monitor the effects
of their thoughts yet. They can learn how the prayer-fields work.
We can help them."

We watched as all the clerics began to walk toward Bill's
house, along with Natalie and Tashi, who were still deeply engaged in conversation.

A moment of skepticism swept over me. Even after all that I'd
seen, I still had my doubts that humans could really empower
angels.

"Do you really think we can summon angels to help ourselves
and others?" I asked Wil. "Would we be given that much power?"

"It's not that easy," he said. "In fact, it is impossible for someone with negative intentions to attempt. None of this works unless we are fully connected within with the energy of the creator,
and sending our energy very consciously out in front of us,
touching others. If we have the slightest bit of ego involved or
anger present, all the energy collapses and the angels can't respond. Do you see what I'm saying? We're God's agents on this
planet. We can affirm and hold the vision of divine will, and if
we authentically get in alignment with that positive future, we'll
have enough prayer-energy to direct the angels to act."

I nodded, knowing he was right.

"Do you see what all this is?" he asked. "All this information,
it's the Eleventh Insight. The knowledge of the prayer-fields takes
human culture a step further. When we understood the Tenth—
that human purpose on this planet was to create an ideal spiritual
culture by holding the vision—something was still missing. We

didn't know how, exactly, to hold it. We didn't know the details of how to use our faith and expectation energetically.

"Now we know. The reality of Shambhala, the secret of prayer-fields, has given us this. We can now hold the vision of a spiritual world and act to bring it about through our creative power. Human culture can't progress further until we consciously use this power in the service of spiritual evolution. We have to do as those in the temples were doing: methodically set our prayer-fields on all those key situations out there that will make the difference. The true role of the media, especially television, is to point out these problem areas. We must notice every discussion, every scientific debate, every struggle someone is having between the dark and the light, and take the time to use our fields."

He looked around. "We can do this in small communities, churches, circles of friends all over the world. But what if the power of every religion was combined into one giant, unified prayer-field? Right now the field is fragmented, even canceled out by negative prayer and hatred. Good people are letting their thoughts add to evil, thinking it doesn't matter.

"But what if that changed? What if we set a field, larger than the world has ever seen, sweeping across the planet to uplift those insidious forces everywhere who want to centralize power and control everyone else? What if every reform group in every profession and occupation knew how to do this? What if an awareness of the field spread that far?"

Wil paused for a moment.

"And what if we all really believed in the angelic realms," he continued, "and knew that it was our birthright to empower them? There's no situation we couldn't immediately affect. The new millennium could look a lot different from how it is now. We would truly be the warriors of Shambhala winning the battle over how the future will look."

He stopped talking and looked at me very seriously. "It is the true challenge of this generation. If we don't succeed, all the sacrifices of the past generations could be in vain. We might not get past the environmental damage that is occurring . . . or the insidious acts of the controllers.

"The important thing," Wil continued, "is to begin to build a conscious, 'thought' network. To link the warriors together . . . Every person who knows has to connect with everyone else in their lives who would want to know."

I was silent. What Wil was saying made me think of Yin and all the others under the Chinese tyranny. What had happened to him? I wouldn't have made it without his help. I told Wil what I was thinking.

"We can still find him," Wil said. "Television is only the precursor to perfecting your mind's eye, remember. Try to find an image of where he is."

I nodded and tried to let my mind go blank, thinking only of Yin. Instead the face of Colonel Chang appeared and I recoiled. I told Wil what had happened.

"Remember the look he had," Wil said, "when he seemed to be waking up, and find that expression in the image."

I found that expression in my mind's eye, then suddenly the image shifted to Yin in a jail cell, surrounded by guards.

"I saw Yin," I said, extending my prayer-energy and empowering the higher realms until the scene grew lighter all around him. Then I visualized the light spreading to all those who were keeping him imprisoned.

"See an angel by Yin," Wil said, ". . . and by the colonel."

I nodded, thinking of the Tibetan code of compassion.

Wil raised an eyebrow and smiled as I concentrated again on the images. Yin would be safe. Tibet would eventually be free.

This time I had no doubt.